NO OTHER HOME

NO OTHER HOME

Living, Leading, and Learning
What Matters Most

MATT BESLER
with Patrick Regan

Foreword by Graham Zusi

Andrews McMeel
PUBLISHING®

CONTENTS

FOREWORD
BY GRAHAM ZUSI

Matt Besler and I began our professional soccer journeys at the same time, in the same city, in the same house. One fateful day in January 2009, the Kansas City Wizards selected both of us in the MLS SuperDraft. A few months later, I was living with Matt in his parents' Overland Park, Kansas, home like their new adopted son.

Fast-forward eight years, and together we have accomplished things I couldn't have possibly imagined when we first met. Lifting the MLS Cup and U.S. Open Cup in front of Sporting Kansas City's Cauldron. Representing our country at the World Cup and Copa America. (Heck, we also managed to find our own places to live.) These special moments transcended my wildest dreams, and Matt was by my side every step of the way.

But Matt is so much more than just a great soccer player. In fact, his impact on my life has been more profound off the field than on it. He is a leader and a role model. He is a selfless teammate and a

loyal family man. He is one of my best friends.

Despite all of the trophies and individual accolades he's won, Matt has never changed. More than anyone I've ever known, he has stayed true to himself: calm, collected, dedicated, and passionate. In many ways, Matt is the same person both on and off the field—someone who always takes positives from difficult situations, someone who pours his heart into everything he does, someone who will always have my back.

We could learn a whole lot from watching Matt play soccer, but the stories, experiences, and words he shares in the following pages transcend the field and extend to all phases of life. Matt's a doer and a thinker. He's not the type to demand attention and shout out advice . . . but what he says—in his quiet way—is well worth reading. I hope you enjoy getting to know my friend in this book. I'm pretty sure you're gonna respect him as much as I do.

—Graham Zusi

"First know yourself, then you will begin to understand why things are as they are, and why life is as it is."

—Leon Brown, former Major League Baseball outfielder

Who I Am

STRONG ROOTS, SIBLING RIVALRIES, AND FINDING YOUR TRUE PATH

"If you want to know who I am, ask me where I came from."

—MB5

WHAT THIS BOOK IS.
AND WHAT IT'S NOT.

Before you get started, it's important to understand a few things.

This is not a typical sports biography. Actually, it's not intended to be a biography at all. I will not be going through my life in chronological order telling you about the time I scored ten goals in a youth soccer game. I don't need to tell you my stats and how many games I've won—you can google that if that's what you want to know. Instead there will be personal stories from my past that taught me something important or useful that I want to share.

When I began this book, I knew I wanted to do something different, something not typically done by professional athletes. The initial inspiration for this book came from a blog post I made a few years ago about how to spend your time.

Honestly, I wrote it without thinking much about the outcome. I figured only a few people would read it, maybe a hundred if I was lucky. However, this particular post caught fire and resonated with many people. (I've included the original post on page 46.) I received tons of positive feedback; it got to the point where people would print a copy of the blog post and ask me to sign it. I even had a teacher come up and thank me, saying that her fifth-grade class did a project based on the post. When she told me how much it had impacted her students, it gave me a feeling I've never had before. If so many people (especially young people) were inspired by what I had written in a simple blog post, why not write more of them?

I did write more of them, and I found that I really liked the process. I was even approached by a few publishing companies about a book deal, but the timing didn't seem right. I wasn't ready to take it that far.

I stuck with my blog, but to be completely honest, it kind of stalled. Actually, it totally stalled. I learned later that that's not unusual. Research shows that 95 percent of blogs are abandoned by their writers within a few months. I'll admit that I missed it. I felt like I had a lot to say, but I also had a lot to do. I could always write more later.

in a journal as therapy for my brain. They told me to write about anything. Naturally, I started writing short journal entries about my experiences, similar to the blog posts I'd written a few years earlier. That's when I knew it was the right time to pursue something like this. That's when I went back to the publishers with my idea.

My plan was to pull together a collection of posts, quotes, autobiographical stories, ideas, and opinions. Not only would this book potentially inspire people,

---

"A goal without a plan is just a wish."
—Antoine de Saint-Exupéry

Then, on March 24, 2016, something hit me: a soccer ball to be exact. I joke, but it was serious. I was struck in the head while practicing with the U.S. Men's National Team. I suffered a severe concussion that sent me to the hospital and put me on the sidelines for several weeks. (I'll come back to this experience later in the book.)

As I started to recover, my doctors recommended that I write

I thought, this project would be therapeutic for me as I worked my way back from the concussion.

My goal isn't to sell millions of copies and make a bunch of money. If I wanted to try and do that, I would have written a traditional biography with juicy details and controversial stories from my career. In fact, I'll be donating a percentage of the proceeds to my charity, the Besler Family Foundation.

Stop "trying"
to be...

Also, my goal isn't to preach. I will not tell you how to live your life, how to be happy, or exactly how to become a professional soccer player. I'm only sharing my experiences and insights because I believe they can help people and guide them in their own life decisions. When I was younger, I wish I would have had a guidebook to help me with the issues I would face in the future.

More specifically, I wish it would have been written by someone who I looked up to, like a professional athlete. That's why I'm doing this. I want kids and their parents to use this as a reference when questions and hard-to-navigate situations arise, whether related to soccer or not.

Don't feel like you have to read this all at once. It's not a novel. Feel free to break it up, skip around, or put it down and go outside to walk the dog or kick a ball. Read one post a day and reflect on it. Read it together with someone.

This book is for everyone; you don't have to be a soccer player

just be!

or even a soccer fan. When you read this book, I hope it makes you laugh, cry, and think. I hope you fold over the corners of pages that you like, and highlight quotes that motivate you. I hope this book speaks to you, and that you can apply some of the lessons I've learned to your own life. Ultimately, I hope you like it enough that when you're done, you pass it along to your kid, a friend, or someone else you think will enjoy it.

MY BACKBONE

Who am I? How would I describe myself? What's important to me? These are questions that are difficult to answer. But they're important questions if you truly want to know someone.

Instead of describing myself with a bunch of adjectives and words I barely understand, I want to try something different. One of my college friends recommended this strategy to "introduce myself." He said it's important to give your audience a backbone for the rest of the book. Understanding who and what influences me will help give you an idea of where I'm coming from.

How do I do that? The best way for me to show you what my backbone is made of is by sharing the six most important aspects that make me who I am.

> Make a list of the five most important people in your life. Then, reach out to each of them and thank them for everything they do for you. You can repeat this once a year or more often if you like. Sometimes it may be hard to pick five; sometimes it may be easy. It's interesting to see how your list changes through the years. It's also a great habit that will make those closest to you feel appreciated.

AMANDA + PARKER

AMANDA AND PARKER: My Wife and Baby Girl

Amanda is by my side through everything, no matter what. She has so many qualities I admire. Mostly, she motivates and challenges me to be a better person. As we share our lives together, I fall in love with her more each day. Parker arrived halfway through the writing of this book. She's given my life more purpose than ever . . . and I fall in love with her more every day, too!

MOM & DAD

My parents, **GREG AND DIANE**, have been with me since day one. I'm very close with my parents and luckily I get to see them almost weekly. They made, and continue to make, so many sacrifices to help get me where I am today. They might not realize it, but I'm still following their lead to this day.

BROTHERS

I have two younger brothers, **MIKE AND NICK**. Both are very athletic, competitive, and talented. Even though we're adults now, I still try to set good examples for them. As we've gotten older, I've found myself looking up to them just as much as they look up to me.

FRIENDS

I'm going to brag. **MY FRIENDS** are awesome. They continue to impress me with their accomplishments. Each of my friends is unique, extremely smart, and driven. They humble me every time we get together, and I strive to be more like them.

CAREER

I want to be successful at whatever I do. Currently, that means putting as much effort as possible into being the best **PROFESSIONAL SOCCER PLAYER** I can be. I'm a big believer in outworking your competition. This is easier said than done, but when you actually do it, good things usually happen.

MAY 28, 2016 USA VS KANSAS CITY, KANSAS

FAITH

You might be surprised that I don't have this higher on my list. As I put together my backbone, I was tempted to put my faith at the top, but I had to be honest with myself. Is faith *the* most constant aspect in my life? I wish I could say yes, but I can't because I'm too inconsistent. However, having a **STRONG FAITH** is important, and it's something I continue to work on. My goal is to move faith higher up my backbone list.

THE YELLOW
BRICK ROAD

'm proud to be the first Kansas native to ever play in the World Cup. As a Kansan—especially one playing the most international sport in the world—you get used to the "clever" *Wizard of Oz* comments from those with limited knowledge of Kansas. "Is your mom named Dorothy?" "How's Toto?" "Did you get here on the yellow brick road?"

But you know what? I'm proud of my roots, and I'm proud to rep my home state. Those comments don't bother me—I always just laugh them off.

I don't know about the yellow brick road, but I do know about the path I've taken and how hard I've worked to stay on track. Some people might look at my background and think my story is boring and uneventful, and I get that. But I also think there's something to be said about staying on course the entire journey. It takes a great deal of determination, focus, and hard work. I was told to "work on your technique, and you'll get a college scholarship." So I worked on my technique by passing the ball against the wall for an hour after school each day. "Work on your speed, and you'll make it to the pros." So I worked on my speed by pushing the sled and running sprints with a parachute behind me. "Work on playing faster, and you'll have a shot at the national team." So I worked on playing faster by limiting myself to only playing with one or two touches during training.

Looking back, there wasn't a standout moment for me. I just put my head down and did what I was supposed to do. If that makes my story boring, then so be it. But in some ways, I actually think it makes my story more interesting. How many times have you heard about someone with unbelievable talent but, for various reasons, never quite made it? I had a plan, stuck to my plan with extreme perseverance and drive, and somehow made it to the level I dreamed about.

I never thought about this before, but there was nothing magical about the yellow brick road. Extraordinary things happened all around it—trees talked, monkeys flew, witches appeared and disappeared—but the yellow brick road was just the path. And it had to be walked, one step at a time.

So, yeah, maybe I did get here on the yellow brick road.

It's important to understand that no two paths are the same. There were twenty-three players who represented the United States at the World Cup in Brazil in 2014, and all twenty-three players traveled a different path to get there. Don't get discouraged if you stray from your path for a moment. Don't be worried if your path isn't as exciting as someone else's. Realize that it's different for everyone. Embrace your path—your own yellow brick road—whatever that may be.

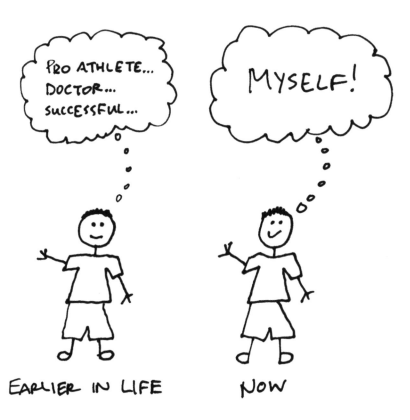

In today's world, there's so much emphasis on image. There are too many comparisons. Quit trying to be someone else. Take a step back from the pressures of trying to fit in and accept who you truly are as a person. Live your life without thinking about how people are reacting to you. Make decisions based on how *you* feel. Be comfortable and confident with who you are.

BROTHERS BEING BROTHERS (I.E., STUPID)

Saying that my brothers and I are competitive is like saying Michael Jordan was good at basketball—the understatement of the century. It's been that way since we were kids, and as we've become older, it's actually gotten worse. It's borderline embarrassing. But we can't help it—I guess it's in our blood.

Whenever the three of us get together, we play some kind of game, or fall into some type of competition. Note that I didn't say "friendly" competition. We are genetically incapable of playing "just for fun." Play Catch Phrase but don't keep score? Yeah, right. Ping-Pong on Christmas Day? Guaranteed to go home sweaty.

"Maybe the journey isn't so much about becoming anything.

Maybe it's about unbecoming everything that isn't really you, so you can be who you were meant to be in the first place."

—Anonymous

My parents could tell endless stories of our competitive natures gone wild, but the "grape story" has become a family favorite.

One night we were having dinner as a family. My parents were outside on our back patio enjoying happy hour while tending the grill. Inside, my brothers and I sat around the kitchen island snacking on some pretzel chips, dip, veggies—just a few appetizers until the main course was ready. There was also a colander full of grapes.

It all started when my youngest brother, Nick, challenged my middle brother, Mike, to a contest. Nick bet Mike he could throw more grapes into a drinking glass that was sitting across the room on our dinner table. Without hesitation, Mike accepted the bet. They each got five grapes and whoever made the most shots won. Both were extremely confident in their abilities. But let me tell you, with the glass all the way across the kitchen, it was not an easy shot.

Neither made a single shot. A combined zero for ten. Normal brothers might have laughed it off and moved on. Not us. The lack of a clear "winner" lit a fire in my brothers—and in me, too. I was pretty sure I could outperform them, so to make things more interesting, I made a bold statement: "All right, first person to make a grape into the glass gets $100!"

It was game on. Of course, we had to alternate turns to make sure we all had an even number of attempts. One by one, we shot. One by one, we missed. There were a few close calls, and a few that "hit the rim" and bounced out. But we kept missing.

A FEW WORDS FROM MOM . . .

I loved that I had all boys. It suited my personality much better than if I had had all girls. I was somewhat of a tomboy growing up . . . I preferred to hang with the boys and enjoyed all of the active competitive games they played. Raising boys came easy to me.

Because of their gender and genetics (both my husband and I are very competitive!), I knew a competitive household was inevitable. Early on it was who could build the tallest building with their blocks before it would topple over. (Probably why they are so good at Jenga now!) Then the video games ruled— who could reach the highest level in Donkey Kong—followed by backyard football, soccer, basketball, and street hockey games. I loved that this competitive spirit kept them physically active and healthy.

Raising three athletic, competitive boys was a joy, but I always stressed the difference between being confident and being conceited. Having a humble attitude did not mean thinking less of yourself, but thinking of yourself less.

—Diane Besler

None of us for one second stopped to think that maybe this wasn't such a good idea. Or that maybe we should just give up—that it wasn't meant to be. No, it had to be done. It was going to be done.

Finally, after about ten minutes of shooting, Mike made it. He erupted with joy and immediately ran around the kitchen celebrating. Nick and I covered our faces with our hands in disbelief. Then the sliding glass door to the back patio opened and my mom walked in.

She couldn't believe what she saw. Actually, none of us could. Over by our dinner table (site of the target glass), there must have been a hundred grapes on the floor. Worse, the wall behind the table was stained from all the shots that went long and smashed into it. In the fog of competition, we didn't realize the mess we were making. We were so locked into winning we didn't notice that we were splattering the wall.

Ten minutes earlier, a nice, fresh bunch of grapes had been sitting in a colander for us to enjoy. (My mom had gone to the store and bought them for us that afternoon.) Now the colander held only a completely plucked grape stem and a few paper towels. We hadn't eaten a single grape. They had all been thrown across the kitchen toward a glass cup . . . all because of a sibling rivalry. (And winning $100!)

The most embarrassing part? This happened in 2012. I was twenty-five years old, Mike was twenty-two, and Nick was nineteen. (And as Mike reminds me several times a year, I still owe him that $100. It's in the mail, Mike.)

This is probably a good time to apologize again to my mom. Although we must've gotten our competitive nature from *somewhere* . . . right?

"My father used to play with my brother and me in the yard. Mother would come out and say, 'You're tearing up the grass.'

'We're not raising grass,' Dad would reply. 'We're raising boys.'"

—Harmon Killebrew,
Baseball Hall of Famer

CLEAR EYES, FULL HEARTS

Do you have one particular quote or mantra you try to live by? One particular saying you find yourself always coming back to?

I do. And, surprisingly, it comes from *Friday Night Lights*, an NBC series about the ups and downs of a small-town Texas football team. If you haven't seen it, watch it. You'll thank me later.

Before Coach Taylor's high school football team goes onto the field each Friday night, he ends his pregame speech with the simple phrase **"Clear eyes, full hearts."** Then his team collectively chants back, **"Can't lose!"**

"CLEAR EYES, FULL HEARTS. CAN'T LOSE!"
It's so simple, but it's so true. This is the one quote I try to live by and this is what it means to me.

CLEAR EYES:

Be in the present moment. Have full concentration. Clear your mind and vision from distraction, stress, and doubt.

FULL HEARTS:

Fill your heart with passion and confidence. Give everything you have.

CAN'T LOSE:

At the end of the day, if you are completely focused and engaged, you can't lose.

Honestly, I'm confident that if I compete in each game with clear eyes and a full heart, I'm going to be successful. And if I still end up losing on the scoreboard (because this happens), it's OK. I can live with it because I can look myself in the mirror and know I gave my all. Playing with clear eyes and a full heart gives me a sense of inner peace, regardless of the outcome. So, basically, **I CAN'T LOSE**.

I challenge you to approach some of the events in your life with clear eyes and a full heart. Whether it's a job interview, a first date, or a gym workout, if you go in with clear eyes and a full heart, you'll believe in yourself. No matter what happens, you won't lose. And trust me, most of the time you'll end up nailing that interview, getting that second date, or crushing your workout.

Enjoy your day . . . I'm going to shovel off my driveway from a snowstorm last night. (I'm writing this in winter in Kansas City.) With clear eyes and a full heart, maybe I can get it done in twenty-five minutes instead of thirty! Push yourself to the limit, always keeping this quote in mind: **CLEAR EYES, FULL HEARTS . . . CAN'T LOSE!**

"Fear and incentives are short-term motivators. Purpose and meaning are long-term."

How I Got Here

INSPIRATION, PERSPIRATION, AND THE GENIUS OF THE POST-IT NOTE

"The best views come from the hardest climbs."

— MB 5

LOSING . . .
AND LEARNING

As I look back on my childhood, it's hard to pinpoint one particular source of my extreme competitiveness. Maybe I was born with it. Maybe it was a combination of a couple different things that influenced me. I don't know exactly how or why it developed. All I know is I

became competitive at a very early age. I learned at seven-years old that I hate losing more than I love winning.

Because I was the oldest child, I was the guinea pig to try out all the different activities and sports. This meant signing up for Cub Scouts. During my first year, the big end-of-the-year project was building a Pinewood Derby car. For a competitive second-grade boy, the Pinewood Derby may as well have been the Super Bowl. The build-up to Derby Day lasted months. The day itself would be an opportunity for me to shine against the fellow kids in my "pack."

From the start, my dad made it clear to me this was *my* car. He would help guide me every step of the way, but he wanted me to do the work. I was already heavily interested in soccer by then, so

I told my dad I wanted to make my car look like a soccer cleat. I spent weeks and weeks sanding, painting, and weighing. Finally, a few nights before the big day, I finished. My masterpiece looked exactly like the soccer cleat I'd cut out of a magazine to use as a model. I couldn't stop smiling because I knew my car was going to be the best. Who else would be cool enough to make their car into a soccer cleat?

The moment I walked into the school gymnasium, my heart dropped. When I looked at all the cars lined up on the table, I couldn't believe my eyes. They looked like professional cars! Lightweight, aerodynamic, perfectly sanded . . . I even saw a dad break out a scale to make some last-minute changes on weight distribution. You've got to be kidding me. Talk about intimidating! Here I was with my soccer cleat

"If you can't accept losing, you can't win."
—Vince Lombardi

I remember waking up that Sunday morning and feeling like it was Christmas. I couldn't wait to race my car. On the drive over to our elementary school where the derby took place, my dad tried to calm me down. "Even if your car isn't the best," he said, "It's still OK. I'm very proud of the work you put in." Yeah, yeah, yeah . . . I rolled my eyes. I thought there was no way my car would lose. I didn't care about being proud of the work I did; I cared about winning. I was confident. (You can see where this is going, right?)

I had designed and completed myself. It was heavy. It was boxy. It stuck out like a sore thumb. But at least it looked like a soccer cleat; I had that going for me.

It was announced that each car would get a guaranteed five races, then the elimination rounds would start, leading to a final race to crown the champion. Before my first race, my heart was beating out of my chest. I don't think I'd felt that kind of adrenaline and nerves ever before. All I wanted was for my car to be fast.

In the first race, I got dead last. In the second race, same thing. In the third race, I got dead last again, and it wasn't even close. By the time the fourth race came, I was in tears. I was embarrassed. I didn't want to race anymore. My dad came over and pulled me aside. I'll never forget what he did next. He looked down at his watch and said, "Matt, do you know what time it is? It's 11:45 a.m. That means we have fifteen minutes before the Chiefs game starts. If we leave now, we can make it back home in time for kickoff. What do you say we go home to watch the game together, and at halftime we can play catch outside?"

That was all I needed to hear. I grabbed my last-place soccer cleat car, and we snuck out the back door without telling anyone.

As I wiped my tears away on the way home, my focus completely shifted from the Pinewood Derby to the Chiefs game. I truly felt special that my dad invited me to watch the Chiefs game with him. I thought, "All those other kids are stuck in the gym racing cars, and I get to go home to watch football with my dad. How cool! I'm the lucky one."

I don't know to what extent this event shaped my personality, but I do know it is one of my strongest childhood memories. As I look back over twenty years later, two things stand out:

1. This was the first time I can remember losing. The first time I remember failing at something among my peers. And I didn't like it. Actually, I couldn't stand it to the point where I had to remove myself from the situation. I believe the feelings I experienced that day ignited my competitive fire.

2. The way my dad handled my disappointment that day is exactly how I want to be with my own kids. He taught me a lesson that day, even if I didn't realize it until twenty years later. He didn't make the day about the derby, or winning, or losing. Or even the Chiefs.

He made the day about me. And that's what mattered most. It's a day I'll remember forever.

Thanks Dad!

MY OLD FRIEND CHIP

Throughout my playing career, I've always carried a big chip on my shoulder. To most people, I may not seem like a guy who would carry a chip, but I promise you it's there. It's been with me a long time and I continue to carry it with me today. When I try to understand exactly where it came from, I keep coming back to the same theme: I've often been overlooked and underestimated.

My career has followed a familiar cycle. With each new stage of soccer (club, high school, college, pro, international) I had to start all over again at the bottom and work my way up. And at the beginning of each stage, I usually went unnoticed for a while. I've never been able to figure out exactly why this is, but it's probably because I'm not a flashy player. That's not who I am.

I'll admit that as a younger player it sometimes frustrated me to be so invisible to coaches. At times, I was tempted to change my approach or to pull a flashy move on the field for the attention. But instead, I continued to play my game, kept my head down, and worked hard. I concentrated on "consistently doing the things I did, well."

Another reason I was often overlooked is I didn't stand out athletically. "Is he fast? Does he have the athletic ability to keep up? Can he jump very high?" These are the questions that usually came up at the beginning of each stage. I've learned to use these questions as motivation. Deep down, these questions light a fire inside me to prove to the doubters that they are wrong.

I made a commitment to show myself and other people that I won't be overlooked athletically.

"Success doesn't always come from the big actions we take, but from the sum of all the small actions we repeat."

—Anonymous

When there's a sprint test (forty-yard dash), I train to get the fastest time. When there's a vertical jump test, my goal is to have the highest score. When we run the beep test, I dedicate and prepare myself to win it and be the most fit. (In case you don't know, the beep test is a fitness test where players run back and forth between two cones that are twenty meters apart. You run from one cone to the other before the beep sounds, and the beeps get faster and faster.) Of course, it doesn't always work out this way. Sometimes another player has a faster time or a better score.

But when I do, I'm not surprised. I expect myself to win because it's what I train for.

Another factor that keeps the chip on my shoulder: It usually takes me more games to win someone over, to gain their trust. I have to consistently perform at a high level before someone pays attention to me. Growing up, this was a bit frustrating. Players with a ton of talent would win everyone over after only one or two games. Not me. This put pressure on me to perform at a high level over and over again. Another frustrating part was that if I did have a bad game (or even a couple) the response was, "He clearly can't play. He's not good enough." Whereas when another player with more talent messed up, the response was, "That's OK. He's young. He's learning. It was just a bad game."

I realize this might sound like I'm griping, but I'm not. I'm just telling it how it was. I probably didn't deserve to get free passes because other players were more talented than me. And the bottom line is, to this day, I'm thankful for the struggles I went through. I wouldn't change them if I could because they force me to consistently perform now, every day. Although I'm "established" as a league veteran, I'm still on edge. I feel like I have to play well every single game, because if I don't, I'll get replaced. That kind of motivation might not be easy to live with . . . but it is effective.

Having a chip on your shoulder can be powerful, if used properly. I've used that chip to give myself a ton of confidence. As a professional, you have to have a very high level of confidence in your own abilities. If someone else doesn't see you the same way you see yourself, you've got to use that as fuel to prove them wrong.

Here are a few other examples of ways I have used the chip throughout my career as motivation:

CLUB SOCCER TEAM: I was a late bloomer, so there were plenty of players ahead of me on my club team, both physically and technically. I never made a dramatic leap ahead of any of my teammates. I kept my head down, consistently worked hard, and gradually progressed. I honestly didn't think about standing out too much at this stage; I just concentrated on playing my own game.

HIGH SCHOOL SOCCER TEAM: Like I said, I was a late bloomer, so my freshman and sophomore year I was way smaller than everyone else. This forced me to rely on technique and intelligence, rather than strength and speed. I'm sure at first I didn't stand out. Actually, I probably stood out for the wrong reasons, like "Why is that tiny kid out there on the field? He's going to get eaten up!" However, I found a way to survive and hold my own. Even if I didn't match up well physically, I learned to compete technically by developing a good first touch and relying on quick reflexes.

Honestly, a lot of it was about survival at that age. I definitely wasn't worried about trying to score goals and stand out. I was more worried about not messing up, not losing the ball, and not getting run over by some senior in the next ten-second period. Eventually, though, I grew and caught up to (and passed) most everyone.

Also, there's always some chatter in high school circles about who's good and who's not. I used to hear things from people at other schools like, "I'm surprised that guy is getting recruited to play D1," and "I don't think he's that good." At times (especially in high school), it was hard not to get caught up in all this. But I realized the only people worth proving something to were my own teammates, so that's what I focused on.

REGION II OLYMPIC DEVELOPMENT PROGRAM TEAM: This was probably the first time I experienced going from being a "star" player (for my high school team) to being a nobody again. I'm not sure why geography matters, but there was not a lot of respect for a kid from Kansas at the regional level.

The region II team was filled with kids from Illinois, Michigan, Ohio, and even Missouri, but no one from Kansas. I knew this, and it made me focus even harder to make the team. My big chip motivated me to show everyone that someone from Kansas could play, too.

COLLEGE TEAM: Most incoming collegiate players will experience this issue. On your high school team, you were "the man," and now you're a highly touted recruit at a Division 1 program. Great, right? But guess what—there are twenty-five other guys on the team who have your same pedigree and most of them are older, more experienced, and probably better than you. So you're forced to adjust your mentality and start over again at the bottom of the ladder. I never got caught up in trying to stand out from the second I arrived on the Notre Dame campus. That wasn't my style. Again, I focused on proving myself to my teammates first, then my coaches, then everyone else.

MLS COMBINE: At the end of the college soccer season, around fifty players get invited to the combine.

At the combine, you play in front of professional scouts and coaches for a few days in hopes of impressing them enough to be drafted. I'm sure a few professional coaches knew my name, but I guarantee most of them didn't—not like they knew the other players there. And I knew this going in. It almost felt like there was nothing I could do to get the coaches to recognize me.

On day one, I played well but wasn't mentioned on anyone's end-of-the-day report or watch lists. I don't think I was included in any mock drafts either. Day two was another great day—still nothing. It's a three-day camp, and most players only got to play two games, but because of some injuries I was asked to play again. I actually was hesitant to play. I had already played two games and did well, so I didn't want to give myself a chance to have a bad game. Plus, my body was extremely sore and tired. Playing three games in three days was almost unheard of at that level and age. I remember talking to my dad on the phone and telling him I had to play one more game. I'm sure he could sense the negative tone in my voice. I wasn't thrilled about having to play again. He said, "Great! Another chance to show what you've got and impress a team. You have nothing to lose!" He was right. It's not like I got noticed that much from the first two days anyway.

I went out and did the same stuff I did the first two games. Personally, I didn't feel like I stood out that much, but deep down I knew I had another very solid game. I must have done something right because sure enough, my agent called me right after and said he started getting calls from almost every team.

PROFESSIONAL TEAM: When I turned pro, there were definitely a lot of questions about whether or not I could compete at that level. I know a lot of people thought I was too small to play the center back position as a professional and that I wasn't fast enough to keep up with the forwards. Those were valid concerns, but I made it a point to prove those people wrong—to prove that I could make it as an "undersized, nontraditional" center back. My attitude was that you don't have to be the biggest player on the field to play center back. As long as you're smart, can read the game quickly, and put yourself in the correct positions, you cannot only compete, you can succeed. I was also able to prove that I was fast enough to keep up with forwards. I'm often described as "deceptively fast," which always makes me chuckle.

NATIONAL TEAM: I was also a late bloomer to the U.S. Men's National Team (USMNT) scene. I was never really in the picture as a youth national team player, and I know a lot of people were surprised to hear I didn't make my debut until age twenty-five. I also played four years of college, which is rare for national team players. Whether or not it was because I was underrated, overlooked, not good enough, too young, or a mix of all those factors, it doesn't matter. What matters is I was able to find a way to get motivated by that old familiar feeling of being overlooked. My friend chip helped push me past my limits. Deep down, I knew that if I was persistent in my training habits and consistent on the field, I would eventually get a chance with the USMNT. That's all I could ask for. Once I finally got that chance, it was up to me to make the most of it.

WHAT ARE YOU PLAYING FOR?
(THE WISDOM OF AUNT MARCIA)

As an athlete, motivation is critical. Why are you playing? What are you trying to accomplish? Who are you representing when you take the field? These questions may seem vague and irrelevant, but if you take the time to truly find the right answer to some of them, you're going to become more focused, more determined, and ultimately more successful.

Some of the most inspiring motivational stories come from athletes who are representing something or someone while they play. One of the most powerful examples is when an athlete experiences a tragedy, such as a family death. I've witnessed many occasions when teammates lose a family member and they become extremely motivated by their situation. They suddenly find a purpose, and they feel obligated to represent that person on the field by honoring his or her life.

The athlete becomes extremely locked in and determined, which leads to playing at a completely different level. It's really amazing and powerful to witness this firsthand.

Examples of this kind of personal motivation are everywhere. All you have to do is look at an athlete's shoes or (in baseball) the underside of his cap. Quotes, Bible verses, initials, words, pictures . . . Some athletes even get tattoos to show what motivates them and who they represent.

Early in my career, I admit that I struggled to find a substantial purpose. I was motivated by survival! Why are you playing? To make a living. What are you trying to accomplish? To be accepted. Who are you representing? Umm, myself. There's nothing wrong with being motivated by some of these. I think it's very natural. But I believe that at some point, if you really want to keep your game at the highest level, it's important to find a motivating factor that's more enduring.

Looking back, I realize that my early motivations were often pretty shallow. I was motivated to impress a coach. I was motivated to receive win bonuses. I was motivated to prove myself to the fans so they would like me and buy my jersey. I was motivated by social media. I felt the need to have a good game so that afterward I could log on to Twitter and see how many positive mentions I got. Heck, I was even motivated by the reporters and bloggers who covered the team. I wanted to play well for them so they would give me good ratings and possibly name me "man of the match." All these motivations caused stress, and stress is one of the biggest enemies of performance. Before games, my mind bounced around like a pinball. I had way too many people I was worried about playing for, and my motivating purpose was totally unclear.

Everything changed for me the day I received an e-mail from my aunt, Marcia Pankratz. My aunt Marcia was a very successful athlete. She played field hockey at the University of Iowa where she was named Iowa Female Athlete of the Year and twice selected All-American. She participated in two Summer Olympic Games (Seoul '88, Atlanta '96) and was co-captain of Team USA from 1985 to 1996. After retiring, she became head coach at the University of Michigan, where she still coaches today, and guided them to the 2001 NCAA Championship.

Needless to say, I looked up to Aunt Marcia. A lot. As an athlete, she was the one who made it possible for me to dream about becoming a professional soccer player. As a person, she instantly brings happiness to a room with her upbeat personality. When I was a kid, I loved bragging to my friends about her playing in the Olympics. Spending time with her in the Athlete Village at the 1996 Olympic Games in Atlanta is one of my favorite memories from my childhood. Watching her gave me a glimpse of what it was like to be an elite athlete.

Surprisingly, up until the e-mail she sent me, we had never really talked as adults about playing professional sports. I really regret that because I realize now how much I could have benefited from her unique perspective.

Anyway, a few weeks after the 2014 World Cup ended, I received this e-mail from Marcia:

Sent: **July 10, 2014**

Subject: **USA #5**

Matt—

Now that the dust has settled a bit, I wanted to congratulate you on an amazing run. . . I also wanted to say thank you for bringing so much excitement and pride to Grandma and Grandpa, your mom and dad, your whole family, and me.

I'm sure the experience was awesome and having Mom, Dad, and Mike in the stands was special. For them and all of us, it actually is so much more than you can imagine.

You have given your entire family an amazing gift—one of overwhelming pride, joy, love, happiness, excitement, hope, patriotism . . .

I remember walking in to my first opening ceremonies at the Olympics in Seoul thinking this is so cool that my mom and dad are in the stands watching this! They are up there wearing red, white, and blue, cheering USA . . . I knew they were having a fun time, but I really didn't understand the depth and magnitude of what they were feeling . . . until now.

Until I watched YOU play I didn't realize how truly amazing it is to watch someone you love have that incredible experience. The elation and pride is almost inexplicable . . .

You gave them this gift . . . something far beyond presents, trophies, championships, and honors.

You have trained so hard, sacrificed and committed yourself to be the best you can be. You are so deserving of all that is in front of you now. I am thankful that you have had this wonderful experience which you have earned. I am even more grateful to you for providing your whole family a memory that will last a lifetime.

Love you,

Marcia

Wow. Words can barely describe what it felt like reading this e-mail for the first time. I don't know how many times I've read it since, but tears come to my eyes almost every time (which doesn't happen often with me). Marcia's words forever changed what motivates me. No longer do I worry about what other people think. I can't control a coach's thoughts. Money isn't as big of a factor as it was. I don't care what people say about me on social media after games. I'm not motivated by trying to prove myself to the "experts."

Once I discovered the shallowness of such motivating factors, it became much easier to focus, relax, and perform. And thanks to Marcia, once I realized what truly motivates me, my purpose was clear.

"Elation and pride . . . you gave them this gift . . . something far beyond presents, trophies, championships, honors . . . You provided your whole family a memory that will last a lifetime . . . "

PRIDE and **FAMILY**. That's why I play. That's who I represent. Always has been. I just hadn't realized it.

THE POWER OF
A SMALL PIECE OF PAPER

I love Post-it Notes. Throughout my career, they've been kind of a secret weapon for me. They're cheap, simple, and come in a range of attractive pastel colors . . . but they are also powerful.

I've used Post-it Notes to motivate myself hundreds of times. Here are just two examples.

First, I'm not a naturally assertive person. Early in my professional career, my coach challenged me to become more vocal on the field. He was looking for me to be more demanding of my teammates—more of a leader. I wanted to achieve this, but I needed extra reminders to help get me there. So I got out a Post-it Note and wrote:

"Be the most demanding, most positive, and hardest working player today. TALK!!!"

I placed it in the center console of my car. Each morning, right before I walked into our practice facility, I would open up my center console and put my wallet away. And each time I did this, I saw the Post-it Note and read what I had written. It didn't matter if I was having a good day, bad day, if it was a rainy day, sunny day . . . each morning when I read that note, it helped put me in the right mind-set for that day's practice. Over time, this mind-set became habit.

The second example is from 2012 when I had one of the best seasons of my career. I ended up winning the MLS Breakout Player of the Year, as well as the MLS Defender of the Year. Because of this,

I was hoping to get my first chance with the U.S. Men's National Team (USMNT) the following January. Unfortunately, when the roster came out, I wasn't on it.

Instead of pouting and feeling sorry for myself, I went to work—with the help of a Post-it Note. I looked at the roster and wrote down all five players in my position who got selected over me. I stuck that note on the wall right next to where I kept my gym bag. Every morning when I went to the gym in the off-season, I would see that Post-it Note and force myself to read the five names who were at the USMNT camp instead of me. I even said their names out loud, which made it harder. Each time I read those names, it lit a fire inside of me. I was angry that I wasn't there and they were. Nothing against those players—I respected them because they all deserved to be there—but I used them as motivation. As a result, I completed one of my most demanding off-season training programs, which set me up to have another solid season. The following year, I received my first USMNT call-up in August. And when the January camp roster came out, my name was on the list.

POST UP!
Put Post-its on your bedside table, on your bathroom mirror, on your dashboard or steering wheel, in your underwear drawer, on your refrigerator, inside your locker . . . anywhere you'll see them often.

" Don't let what you want now get in the way of what you want most. "

PASSION
OR PASSING INTEREST?

There is a difference between an interest and a passion. An interest is something you enjoy and find the time to do when you can. A passion is something you're willing to sacrifice for and make a priority in your life.

"So Matt, what do you like to do outside of soccer? What are your other interests?"

I get asked that question a lot, and I always have a difficult time answering.

Unlike a lot of my friends who have major interests outside of their jobs—things such as hunting, golf, barbecue, cars—nothing jumps out at me.

It's not because I'm boring or have no life outside of soccer. It's because playing soccer at the professional level requires huge sacrifices, which means my outside interests often take a back seat.

My passion to be successful in soccer is more important than any interests outside of that. Sure, I still have interests—hanging out with friends, watching sports and Netflix, listening to country music, traveling, playing Ping-Pong, reading, even writing this book—but never at the expense of soccer. Soccer will always take precedence. It's a passion. The others are simply interests and will always be sacrificed.

It's been this way for a long time. In high school, like any normal teenager, I had a lot of things going on—a lot of interests. I was interested in playing FIFA and NCAA Football on Xbox, flirting with girls, going to the pool in the summer, and staying out late with friends. But I was passionate about playing Division I soccer at a prestigious university. That passion drove me and kept me focused. And in order to achieve that passion, I had to be willing to make some sacrifices.

My junior year in high school I dated a girl, Lainey, and prom was approaching. It was the first time we were allowed to go to prom, so everyone was excited. There was a buzz around our class for weeks—discussion of dresses, dinners, after-parties, all that good stuff. My group of friends even decided to get a limo for the night. I was really looking forward to taking Lainey to prom, but there was one problem. That same weekend, I had a soccer tournament in Cincinnati.

Now, a lot of people might have skipped the soccer tournament in favor of attending prom. That's totally understandable. Prom only happens once in your life (well, twice if you go as a junior and a senior), and I had been to hundreds of soccer tournaments before. But remember, my passion was trying to play collegiately, and this tournament had the potential to help me do that. As much as I wanted to attend prom, I knew it wasn't as important so I decided to go to Cincinnati for the soccer tournament. At the time, it was a hard decision to make because I truly felt like I was missing something special. I was also jealous. Lainey ended up getting asked to prom by another guy (a friend), which was difficult to handle as well. My true passion really got tested that weekend.

In the end, everything worked out (like most things do). I went to the soccer tournament, and the disappointment of missing prom didn't last very long at all.

Is it a coincidence that I wound up playing college soccer at Notre Dame? Or that I'm still getting to play as a professional? Maybe, but I don't think so. I'm not saying my life would have been completely different had I decided to skip that tournament and go to prom. What I *am* saying is that my decision showed the depth of my commitment. Sure, I might have still ended up a pro if I had blown off that one tournament. But if I'd been willing to skip that one, it's likely that I would have also been willing to miss other tournaments because of social events, or to have more time to hang out with friends. The sacrifice and passion go hand in hand. If you're not willing to endure the former, you probably don't have the latter.

If you're a kid, a teenager, or a young adult, you're going to face dilemmas like these. The earlier you recognize your passions, and realize you'll have to sacrifice some of your interests to achieve those passions, the easier it will be to make the tough decisions when the time comes.

I'm not saying you shouldn't have any interests outside of your passion. Of course you should. You should still hang out with friends, stay up late, go to parties, play video games . . . whatever it is you like to do. But don't let those get in the way of your passion.

WHAT DO YOU WANT MOST?

Make a list of the five things you want most in your life, ranked from first to fifth.

When a conflict comes up, ask yourself, "Will doing this now take away from one of the items on my list?" If the answer is yes, you'll have to decide if it's worth it or not. Also, it's a good idea to make a new list each year, because sometimes items on your list will change.

CURRENT LIST:

1. Be a good father and husband

2. Soccer

3. Provide financial stability for my family

4. Be healthy

5. Find ways to get involved in the community

RETRO LIST
(FROM HIGH SCHOOL)

1. Soccer scholarship

2. Girlfriend

3. Have fun with friends

4. Gas money

5. Earning an A in calculus

TIME: INVESTING OR SPENDING? (MY INVESTMENT IN MLS CUP 2013)

Several years ago, I watched a *60 Minutes* special on Nick Saban, the head football coach at the University of Alabama. The following is something he said to a group of young football campers:

"When you **INVEST** your time, you make a goal and a decision of something that you want to accomplish. Whether it's make good grades in school, be a good athlete, be a good person . . . Whatever it is you choose to do,

you're investing your time in that.

"When you **SPEND** your time, you play Xbox. That's spending time. It accomplishes nothing. And I know all of you would say, 'Oh, man, I need to have my relaxation time.' You know what I say to that? And excuse me to all the mamas out here, but that's bull—. You don't need to do that."

Fast forward to December 2013 . . . I was mindlessly scrolling through a random acquaintance's

Instagram photos . . . all of them. It took me thirty minutes! Then I realized I didn't even really know the person. What was I doing? I immediately thought about Nick Saban and his message to those young football campers.

I was just spending my time. I was accomplishing nothing. There's no true value in what I was doing, nothing to help my future success and happiness. So right then, I logged off Instagram. I thought about how I wanted to invest my time. What did I want to accomplish?

My short-term goal was clear enough—to win the MLS Cup that was just a few days away. It's something my teammates and I had been working toward for a very long time. This is what I had invested my time in. But I needed to keep investing!

So instead of spending time on Instagram, I watched game tape of Real Salt Lake (our opponent in the MLS Cup). I stretched by foam rolling. I hydrated myself by drinking water. All of these investments were made to prepare me to succeed, in hopes of winning the MLS Cup.

Thank you, Nick Saban. You helped me become more focused. Your words reminded me that I must dedicate myself in every way possible to accomplish my goals.

Remember, you have a choice what you do with your time—invest wisely!

Investing your time means spending it for a worthwhile purpose: to work toward something, to accomplish something that will help you achieve your goal.

Some players—or teams—spend two hours in the afternoon sleep-walking through drills and going through the motions of practice. But others invest their two hours by working hard, correcting mistakes, and improving on each play. The difference between spending time and investing time can impact results dramatically.

It's about quality of time, not quantity.

"Everyone at the next level starts from scratch. You will have to prove yourself again. It's all about what can you do now; it's about what you are going to do going forward!"

Moving Up

LEARNING, LEADING, AND TAKING
YOUR GAME TO THE NEXT LEVEL

"Never be satisfied.
Always ask yourself,
'What's next?' You'll
have plenty of time to
sit back, relax, and think
about it all one day."

—MB5

DREAMS, DOUBTS, AND THE DANGER OF THE BACKUP PLAN

Becoming a professional soccer player was always a dream of mine, but it was never a clear dream. What I mean is I didn't dream of becoming a professional soccer player, specifically. All I ever wanted was to become a professional athlete in general. I didn't care if it was in soccer, basketball, baseball, football, hockey, or golf. In school when everyone had to write down what they wanted to do when they grew up, I always wrote "pro athlete." Somewhere along the way, I narrowed it down to soccer. I guess I wasn't big enough for football or tall enough for basketball, and I didn't have the patience for baseball.

Growing up, I heard the words "backup plan" constantly. I would hear it from my parents, my coaches, my teachers—basically anyone older than me trying to give advice. I would tell them I was going to be a professional soccer player, and then they would remind me that not many people make it that far in sports, and that it's important to have another plan for the "real world" in case soccer didn't work out. One time, in sixth grade, I had to write a three-page report (equivalent to a full-length novel at that age) on what I wanted to be when I grew up. I didn't need to think very hard about that one! Professional soccer player—duh. But as I was walking out of class that day, my teacher said, "Matt, you're not allowed to write about becoming a professional soccer player. You have to pick something else for once." I can't recall what I wrote about . . . go figure.

As I got older I started realizing the advice I received about having a backup plan made a lot of sense. So my mind-set started shifting a bit, especially in high school. I became self-conscious about wanting to become a professional soccer player. I didn't want people to think I was so set on this far-fetched dream of mine that I wasn't in touch with reality. So I started answering questions differently when it came to my future. Instead of talking about soccer first, I would mention something more modest and realistic. My typical answer to "What do you want to do when you get older?" was now something like, "Well, I can see myself going to business school or

"I recall talking about how few people would ever have the chance to play professional sports, and saying that if you were fortunate to have the opportunity that you should pursue it with all the gusto you had."

—Dr. Greg Besler (my dad)

"HAVE A BACKUP PLAN, BUT NEVER STOP DREAMING AND EXTENDING YOURSELF OUT OF YOUR COMFORT ZONE. DON'T LET YOUR BACKUP PLAN GET IN THE WAY OF YOUR DREAMS."

even becoming a doctor. I'd like to play soccer as long as I can, but I know the chances of making it to the highest level are small."

Geez, I just cringe when I remember what I said. I hate that answer. I don't understand why I became so guarded about what I wanted to do. So what if I wanted to become a professional soccer player? Why was I willing to give someone else so much power over my future dreams? They didn't know me. They didn't know what I truly wanted to become or what I felt deep down inside.

Let me interrupt myself to say that having a backup plan is not bad advice. It's actually great advice. In fact, I catch myself telling younger players all the time to make sure they have a backup plan! (And, yes,

I have to laugh at myself for doing this.) What I *am* saying is don't let your backup plan get in the way of your dreams. A backup plan should be exactly that . . . a BACKUP. It should be safe—something to fall back on in case what you really want to happen doesn't work out. Have a backup plan, but never stop dreaming and extending yourself out of your comfort zone. Always have something on the horizon that you're shooting for.

Looking back, if I could redo my high school answer, I would say, "You know what, I'm going to put everything I have into becoming a professional soccer player because it's truly a dream of mine. I know I'll encounter a lot of doubters, but I have a strong feeling I can do it. And if it doesn't work out, I'm going to put myself in a position where I can attend a business or medical school." Boom, that's an answer right there—ambitious but honest.

In college (especially my first two years), I became even more focused on my backup plan. I think it was human nature for me to do that. I was at a very prestigious and academically demanding university where a lot of your time and energy went into setting yourself up for future success in the "real world." You're a product of your environment, right? Well, the environment at Notre Dame dictated that you get good grades, do summer internships at Fortune 500 companies, crush your interview, and get hired full-time by your spring semester senior year. That's what 90 percent (or so it seemed) of my classmates did, so why shouldn't I? I clearly had this mind-set for a while in college. That's not to say I didn't take soccer seriously. I did. I loved soccer. I still put everything I had into becoming the best player I could be. It's just that my backup plan started creeping up, getting closer and closer to my DREAM.

Until one day my junior year when a light bulb went off in my head. I was sitting in my living room with a few teammates—Luke Seibolt, Terry Lee, and Cory Rellas—watching March Madness. There was an NCAA commercial that came on. "There are over 380,000 student athletes, and most of us will go pro in something other than sports." Cory looked over at all of us and said, "I think they're talking about us, guys. Well, everyone except for Bes . . . he's got a chance to be on the other side of that statistic."

Once I heard that commercial, and heard what Cory said, my mind-set completely changed. It was like that commercial was sent down from God, and he was speaking directly to me. Over the next couple of days, we must have heard that commercial fifty times, and each time I heard it, it spoke to me even more. That moment, I made a conscious decision to dedicate myself entirely to becoming a professional athlete. I would use that disheartening statistic as motivation to become the exception. I would also use the encouragement of my classmates and teammates who probably weren't going to get that chance. Not only was I doing this for myself, I was doing this for my best friends. I felt pressure to not let them down.

After all, they were counting on me.

Once I made this conscious decision, I felt relieved. I gained clarity and focus. It became easier to work on getting better, to push myself out of my comfort zone. Instead of worrying about a lot of different things, I could put all my energy into one . . . becoming a pro. Of course, I still maintained my grades, and I also continued to network for jobs, just in case . . . but I was no longer clouded by my backup plan. Thanks to that NCAA commercial, my dream became cemented back at the top of my list where it belonged.

Even after making that decision, I still encountered challenges and periods of doubt. In my senior year, I had a very serious conversation with my parents about my future. My classmates and peers were all beginning to line up interviews with medical schools while also studying for the MCAT, and yet again I felt the need to keep up with them. I spoke to my parents on the phone. I explained to them how I was having trouble deciding when to take the MCAT, picking what medical school to visit during the spring semester, and finding extra time to study. All this on top of trying to have the best soccer season possible, to make my dream come true. There was also a decent chance I wouldn't even be on campus second semester because I would graduate early (after three and a half years) and get drafted by an MLS team. So why even prepare for the MCAT or med school when it may not even happen?

I felt like I was being forced to live two separate lives. I was trying to juggle two completely different paths at the same time. Trying to become a professional athlete is hard enough by itself. So studying for the MCAT and trying to apply to medical schools at the same time was crazy. Yikes! No wonder I was stressed.

Finally, my parents calmed me down. They said, "It seems like you have a lot going on in your life right now and you're at a crossroads. Whatever you end up pursuing, we support you 100 percent and we know you'll be successful. But it's important to understand something . . . from the first time you talked, walked, went to school, started playing, it's all been about becoming a professional athlete. Way back when you were five years old, our neighbors used to tell us, 'I can't believe how good that kid is at kicking a ball . . . he's gonna be a pro soccer player one day.' This dream of yours has always been a big part of your life. Why should it stop now? Go for it!"

It's hard to explain how much this conversation meant to me. After hanging up the phone, I remember feeling like the weight of the world was lifted off my shoulders. I kept smiling to myself and thinking about how our neighbors predicted I would become a professional one day . . . it pumped me up!

My parents convinced me to put my academic life on hold and fully pursue my career in soccer. I stopped studying for the MCAT and started extra training in the gym. I stopped reaching out to contacts about medical school interviews and started setting up meetings with agents. My parents gave me the confidence to not worry about what everyone else was doing at the time and go for my dream.

Looking back, I'm finally starting to realize how special my parents' advice was. It would have been easy for them to push me in a direction away from soccer, but they didn't. They always left that door open for me because they knew it was my dream. And when I needed a little extra push through that door, they were right behind me to help just like they have always been. (Love you, Mom and Dad!)

Sometimes before the biggest matches, I get text messages from various people wishing me good luck. The ones that mean the most are the ones that aren't about soccer. If my brother says, "Hey, good luck in the game tonight," it's not going to mean as much as if he says, "Proud of you for everything you've done already! Have fun and enjoy it. Can't wait to see you next weekend." This immediately gets my mind off the game. And I know that whatever the outcome, I'm still going to see my brother next weekend. This calms me . . . and being calm means playing better.

MAKING THE JUMP

Whether you're jumping from recreational to premier, club to academy, high school to college, or college to professional, here's something to remember: Forget about what you've already accomplished.

Sorry to burst your bubble, but it doesn't really matter anymore. You aren't owed anything for your accomplishments at the previous level. Nothing will be given to you for what you've done. You will have to prove yourself all over again.

That's because everyone at the next level starts from scratch. Your previous résumé is wiped clean. The quicker you realize this, the better off you're going to be.

Many players have a difficult time understanding this transition. They feel a sense of entitlement, which makes it very difficult for them to face a challenge. And trust me, you will be faced with challenges at the next level.

I've experienced this at every level. I've felt entitled before. Don't worry if you do, too . . . it's a natural feeling. When you accomplish something, you're going to feel like you deserve a reward for it. As a freshman in high school, part of me assumed I would make the varsity team right away because I played for a good club team and was on the regional and state Olympic Development Program (ODP) teams. I quickly learned that would not be the case. I ended up having to earn my spot, just like every other player did.

Moving from high school to college was also a difficult transition. As I was graduating high school, I felt like I was on top of the world. State championship, Gatorade Kansas Player of the

Year, All-American, you name it. So when I went off to college to play at the next level, I had a lot of expectations for myself, and I felt like I definitely deserved to play as a freshman. When you move to the collegiate level, though, everyone else has usually accomplished the same things you have. My entire recruiting class was made up of state champions, players of the year, and All-Americans. What I had accomplished didn't matter anymore because it didn't make me special. It was going to get me nowhere at Notre Dame.

My achievements especially didn't matter to the upperclassmen and the existing members of the team. They honestly didn't care how many state championship rings I had and what I did against my high school competition. It's all about what can you do now. Can you compete at the next level? Can you help the team?

So that's what you have to teach yourself. When you jump to a new level, tell yourself it's not about what you've already done, it's about what you are going to do going forward! Stop focusing on past accomplishments and put all your energy into what's ahead.

This will be a difficult mind-set to achieve, especially at the beginning, because there's a good chance you've been surrounded by a lot of people telling you how great you are up to now. I can't tell you how many times I've seen this happen. A player moves on to the next level, doesn't play right away, faces some challenges, calls home to complain, and the parents can't believe it. The parents will say: "Doesn't the coach know you're a state champion? What is the coach thinking? You have to play, for crying out loud . . . you scored thirty-three goals last season as a high school senior!"

Sorry, but it doesn't work like that. Everyone starts fresh when they move to the next level, so reconcile yourself to that fact as quickly as you can.

Parents, this message is for you, too. When your kid moves on, you too have to hit the reset button. Don't keep looking back on what your kid has already achieved—no matter how great it was. It's not going to help him or her at the next level. Be positive and pleasant, but keep them looking forward. That's the direction they're going, after all.

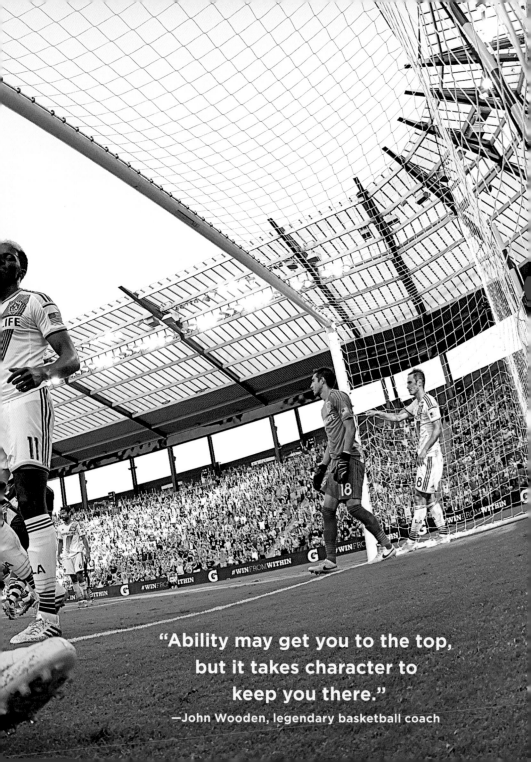

"Ability may get you to the top,
but it takes character to
keep you there."
—John Wooden, legendary basketball coach

SUCCESS ISN'T OWNED. IT'S RENTED.

It's obvious to say that most people enjoy the feeling of success. I do, too! That's why I constantly try to find it in everything I do. Earlier in my life, I sometimes felt that I wanted success more than my peers did. But as I've gotten older and progressed through the professional soccer ranks, I've realized that everyone else around me wants success, too; they have the same level of desire. And each player is doing everything he possibly can to help his team succeed. After all, it's our job. Our livelihood is at stake!

Therefore, if you want to separate yourself from others, you must find something other than success to focus on. Think about it—everyone loves winning championships, lifting trophies, celebrating with champagne, and attending parades through the city. Loving these won't make you different from anyone else you're competing with or against.

Instead, focus on the *process* of success, not success itself. Don't put so much emphasis on the end product. Rather, think about all the little things you must do in order to get there. Fall in love with things like preseason runs, extra weight sessions, breaking down film, yoga sessions, and ice baths. These are the details that will separate you from others. If you fall in love with the details, the end product of success will take care of itself.

There's another advantage to having a "process" mentality over an "end product" mentality. The process will give you much greater satisfaction than the end product. For example, you may work ten months to win a championship, but you'll only get to enjoy it for about two months until the next season starts and you have to begin all over again. Lifting a trophy is temporary. It's a sign of recent success, but it doesn't last. If you want lasting success, it's all about the journey of getting to that championship.

Embrace the journey. Fall in love with the process. It will make the champagne taste a lot sweeter!

of grasp the last few seasons, so finally winning it together was a major high. As he approached me, I expected him to say something like, "Finally! Congrats! Let's go celebrate!" Instead, he said, "Nice work . . . Now we have to win Champions League." I was completely taken aback by this. Just minutes after hoisting the MLS Cup trophy, the Champions

"Success is not owned. It's rented. You have to make deposits on your rent payment every single day."

Immediately after Sporting KC won the MLS Cup in 2013, I remember being in the locker room celebrating together. At first, it was just the players, but after fifteen minutes or so, other members of our organization came in to join the celebration. I remember seeing Robb Heineman, one of our owners, out of the corner of my eye, and he approached me with one of the biggest smiles I have ever seen on him. We had been together at the club for five years and the MLS Cup had slipped out

League trophy was the *last* thing on my mind. But that wasn't the case with Robb. He wanted more. It was clear that night he wasn't truly in love with the end product—the instant success of a championship. He was in love with the process of a championship. And as soon as we got our hands on the MLS Cup, he wanted to start that process over again with another trophy. The more I think back to that night and what he said to me, the more I respect his mentality. It made me want to win more.

Robb, thank you for saying that to me that night. You helped me realize that if you want to consistently find success in sports, you must adopt the process mentality. But I'm always going to give you a hard time for not even enjoying the trophy for five minutes before asking me, "What's next?"

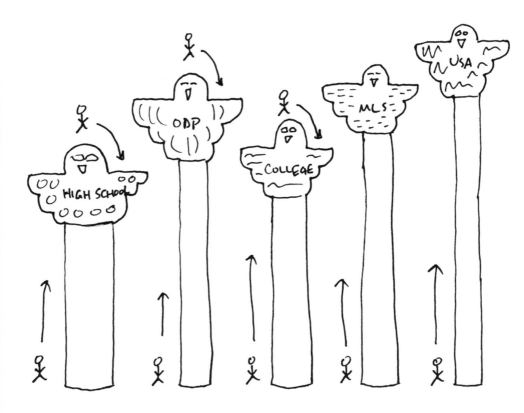

MY "TOTEM POLE" CAREER

My career has been a cycle of totem poles. Bottom of the pole, climb to the top, jump off, and start all over again on a new pole. Repeat.

Here's what I say to myself right before kickoff:

"This is just another game. That's all it is. Remember how many times you've done this before."

PREGAME PEP TALK

t's hard not to be anxious and nervous before a game, but saying the phrase from the previous page helps me relax. No matter the situation—World Cup, MLS Cup, regular season, preseason—I'm simply getting ready to go out and "play another game." That's all it is. To the outside world, certain games might seem and feel bigger than others. But to me, they're all the same. I've played hundreds of games before and the one I'm about to play is no different. I know exactly what to do. I've done it before. Now is the time to enjoy the moment, give everything I have, and be confident.

You might see me with a grin on my face right before kickoff, or even catch me laughing. It's not because I'm not taking the game seriously, or I don't have my game face on. It's because of what I just told myself. I'm realizing, "This is

just another game. That's all it is." I'm remembering how many times I've already done this. I'm about to go and play. I'm about to have some fun.

Over the past few seasons I've found myself saying this to teammates, too. They probably think it's a little weird, but that's OK. I remember saying this to a teammate halfway through the 2015 U.S. Open Cup Final. An injury caused one of our rookies, Saad Abdul-Salaam, to come in at left back, a position he'd never played before. As he made his way onto the field, I went over to him with a smile and said, "We got this. Remember, this is just another game. That's all it is." He probably said to himself, "Who is this guy? Is he crazy? Just another game? Yeah right, this is the U.S. Open Cup Final! And I've never really

played this position before at the professional level."

But I truly meant it. Even though the stakes were high and Saad had never been in that position before, it was just another soccer game. At the end of the day, that's all it was. All he needed to do was make the same plays that he'd made over and over before. I have no idea if what I said to him made any impact on his mind-set—maybe not. But maybe it helped him relax or gave him just a little extra confidence. What I do know is he did an unbelievable job coming into that situation and getting the job done. He played great, and we eventually went on to win the Cup in penalty kicks.

"Lord, I know today is Your plan. I'm giving it to You, and You're going to handle the nerves and stress, because You're the one who is in charge. You're the one who is plowing the field, and at the end of the day, I owe You everything. You're going to be the one who decides how today goes, and therefore I don't have any of the pressure. There is nothing for me to worry about. I'm just trying to live (and play) today as best I can, but all the weight is on You. Please take care of me."

PREGAME PRAYER
I say this prayer to myself before every game. It was inspired by Tim Tebow.

THE ARMBAND:
THOUGHTS ON LEADERSHIP

Throughout my career, I've always found myself in some type of leadership role. It's never something I've sought out or even spent much time thinking about—I've always just wanted to win, and I guess that meant trying to lead others. Naturally, I did most of my leading by example, not necessarily by communicating.

Anytime I've been a captain for a game, I view the opportunity as a privilege. I've been fortunate to experience being captain in club soccer, high school, college, and the pros. Most recently, I've had the honor of being a captain for Sporting KC. I take an enormous amount of pride each time I get to lead our team out of the tunnel. Doing this for the first time in my hometown will always be one of the greatest moments of my career.

Being a captain has taught me a lot about myself and about others. It's not an easy responsibility to take on, and it challenges you in ways that can be very revealing. Early on as captain for Sporting KC, I learned that one of the most challenging aspects of being captain was my own tendency to be too hard on myself. I'm already hard on myself as it is, but when I became a leader, I took being critical of myself to a whole different level—to where it was negatively affecting me. I wanted the team to win so badly that when we didn't, I felt personally responsible. I felt like I had let the team down and I wasn't doing my job. Not only did I feel like I let my team down, I felt like I also let our fans down, our owners down, and our city down. After a loss, I wouldn't sleep well for days thinking about what I could have done

Leadership is positively influencing one person. This is breaking it down to its simplest meaning. If you can think about leadership this way, it becomes less daunting. Don't worry about leading one hundred people, or even eleven. Focus on positively influencing one person. As it becomes more natural to you, your influence will gradually grow.

differently as a leader. I asked myself so many questions: Why did we lose? Were we not prepared? Was our warm-up not good enough? Were we confident? Did we have the right mentality entering the game? Could I have said something different in the pregame huddle?

I was second-guessing myself, not because I wasn't confident in myself or my team, but because I was putting so much pressure on us to win every game. And, of course, you're not going to win every game. I had to find a way to move on quicker and start focusing on the next game, even when we lost. This took time and practice. Unfortunately, I don't have any groundbreaking strategies to achieve this. I just got through it with more experience. Ultimately, I think it's about finding the right balance. Of course it's OK to be upset after losing (you should be), but you also have to take a step back and think about the bigger picture. In a situation when your team comes up short and you feel that weight of responsibility, tell yourself, "This game is over with. My team doesn't need me to be upset for days. My team needs me to start looking forward, NOW."

EIGHT GREAT LEADERSHIP LESSONS

My insights on leadership come not only from my personal experience as a veteran player and team captain, but also from closely observing leaders I admire. Here are eight lessons I've learned:

1. LEAD ACTIVELY.

If you're in a leadership position, you have to constantly learn and adapt. People, circumstances, and environments change, therefore you must be open to evolving and doing whatever is most beneficial at any given moment. If you simply stay the course, you will eventually become ineffective.

2. KNOW YOUR AUDIENCE.

Who are you trying to lead? Different people are motivated differently. For example, I know I have been more subtle and constructive when I'm dealing with someone more sensitive, than I have been with someone thick-skinned. The most effective leaders are the ones who are smart enough to figure out how to tailor their message and style to each person on their team to get the best results.

3. DELEGATE.

No one can lead on their own (even if they think they can). The most successful teams I've been on didn't have one or two clear leaders . . . they always had a bunch of people taking different roles and responsibilities. If you don't have multiple people stepping up and helping, it's probably not going to work. If you play sports and are named a captain of one of your teams, I suggest immediately finding a few others to help. Tell them, "I need your help this season.

We must do this together."
Conversely, if you're not a captain
(and want to win), I suggest you
go up to the captain and offer your
help. Tell him or her, "I'm here for
you, for whatever you need. Let me
know how I can help."

4. LEADERSHIP TAKES WORK.

Know that you must put time
and effort into leading. It doesn't
happen with the snap of your
fingers. Leadership will come more
naturally to some, but no matter
who you are, you can always

get better. Leadership is a skill. It's
something you can work on and
practice, just like on-the-field skills.
One of the best ways to learn is
from other leaders. Biographies
about leaders can be amazing
references!

5. TAKE RESPONSIBILITY.

One of the biggest requirements
of leaders is to take responsibility.
When something goes wrong, step
up and be the first one to raise your
hand. There's no shame in failing
. . . you're going to at some point.

> **"AS A PLAYER MATT JUST QUIETLY LED THE TEAM BY EXAMPLE. HE NEVER SOUGHT THE LIMELIGHT BUT SOMEHOW IT DESERVEDLY FOUND HIM. HE WAS ALWAYS ON TIME, ALWAYS GOT GOOD GRADES, AND NEVER CAUSED A BLINK OF TROUBLE."**
>
> —Bobby Clark, *Notre Dame soccer coach*

6. GIVE CONFIDENCE TO OTHERS.

I think the greatest gift a leader can give someone else is the confidence to succeed. Understand, you might have to do this in different ways with different people, but find a way! As a captain, one of my most important goals leading up to a game is making sure the team is confident. Imagine a team full of confident players! From my experience, when our team plays confidently and to our potential, we can beat anyone. Confidence is the greatest performance enhancer in sports!

7. BE YOURSELF.

If you're not a RAH-RAH speech guy before the game, let someone who is take on that role. If you like to joke around and pull pranks on guys, do it. Don't all of sudden become serious just because you're in a leadership position. Find what comes natural to you and excel in those areas!

8. LEAD BY EXAMPLE.

I shouldn't have to explain this one. It's the most important. Practice what you preach!

"Sports can provide great triumphs, but they can also be humbling. I've learned more lessons from sports than anything else. Discipline, perseverance, responsibility, and work ethic are life-long virtues."

On the Pitch

GOOD TEAMMATES, BAD IDEAS, AND AN INSIDE VIEW OF LIFE IN THE LEAGUE

"Instead of being remembered for any great moments on the field, I'd rather be remembered as a great competitor and an even better teammate."

— MB 5

I GOT YOUR BACK—
AND YOUR SHOES
(HOW TO BE A GOOD TEAMMATE)

On March 26, 2013, the U.S. Men's National Team went down to Mexico City and achieved a historic result. For only the second time ever, we earned a World Cup qualifying point on Mexican soil—a 0–0 tie. I was fortunate enough to be a part of this match. It will be a match I will never forget, for many different reasons.

One day before the match, we trained at Azteca Stadium so we could get used to the field. To be honest, I wasn't thinking too much about the game itself. I was just soaking up the experience. *Estadio Azteca* is an honest-to-goodness temple of soccer—site of two World Cup finals ('70 and '86) and some of the sport's legendary moments including Maradona's famous "Hand of God" goal. It's also massive, with a 100,000 seating capacity. So needless to say, it was a lot to take in.

Of course, I was primarily focused on helping the team prepare, but it's hard not to look around in awe the first time you walk into a historic stadium like that. Plus, there was little chance I would play the following day. Why? It was a massive game, and I was the least experienced player on the roster at the time. I had only played in one game with the squad before, a fairly meaningless friendly against Canada a few months prior. Also, our team had just gotten a big result a few days before—a shut-out win against Costa Rica. So there wasn't much cause to make a bunch of changes, especially in the backfield.

All that changed about fifteen minutes into practice. Clarence Goodson, a veteran center back who had started the previous match and played great, went down with a hamstring pull. Afterward I could see our coach contemplating his options. To replace Clarence, he could move our right back over into the center because he's played both positions before, or he could pull our defensive midfielder back to center back for the same reason. *Or* he could insert me into that spot since I was a natural fit to that position.

Sure enough, he called my name from across the field, so I ran over and joined up with the starting group. From that moment up until kickoff, I couldn't stop thinking about the game and the opportunity. This was my chance.

I got back to the hotel and realized it was going to be a long twenty-four hours leading up to the game. If I continued thinking so much, I was going to work myself up into a frenzy. I was already going to be more nervous than I'd ever been before. I needed to take every measure I could to calm myself down. Usually, I tell my loved ones and trusted friends if I'm playing the following day, just so they know what to expect. But for this game, I decided against it. I knew if I told them, it would increase the pressure I was feeling.

(I bet they were all shocked when they turned on the TV and saw that I was starting.) Additionally, I still wasn't convinced I was going to play. Judging from practice, I was the initial choice to fill in, but I thought our coach could easily change his mind before kickoff and go with someone else.

It wasn't until the next morning, game day, when I officially found out I was starting. From that moment, I had roughly seven hours to kill before kickoff. I tried my best not to think about the magnitude of the game, but it was impossible. My mind was racing. Was I ready? What if we lost? What if I gave up a goal? Would I ever get another chance after this? How many people were going to be watching back home?

On game day, it's standard for the players to bring down their gear, especially their cleats, to the equipment room so the kit man (equipment manager) can pack them and bring them to the stadium. Because I was so new to the group, I didn't know about this. It wasn't part of my routine, and before the game I forgot to bring my cleats down. (Or maybe my mind was in other places!) When

I realized that I had forgotten, I rushed downstairs with my cleats, but unfortunately our kit man had already packed up and left for the stadium. Oh well, I guess I would just have to bring my cleats myself. "Whatever you do, don't forget your cleats!" I kept saying over and over again for the next few hours.

About two hours before kickoff, it was time to leave the hotel for the stadium. I was ready. I had done enough thinking. Now it was time to play. To be honest, my mind was finally at ease. I accepted the challenge and was desperately looking forward to the opportunity of playing. Deep down, I knew I was going to go out and make the most of the chance. I was going to go for it, and play like I had nothing to lose!

This relaxed, confident state of mind wavered a bit when we pulled up to Azteca Stadium. Right away, I felt the hostility and the hatred. The streets were lined with thousands of Mexican fans screaming at us and throwing things at our bus. I'd never seen so many middle fingers in my life! It was hard to not be a little nervous at that moment. Still, I was doing my best to not show it. I kept telling myself, "Be calm. Be cool. Act like you've been here and done this before."

After we got off the bus and started walking down the tunnel to the locker room, I realized I forgot my cleats on the bus. Crap! Of course this would happen. I was obviously a little nervous and forgot them. This could be disastrous . . . and really embarrassing. I panicked.

I spun around to run back to get them, and saw Clarence Goodson right behind me. Holding up my cleats, he calmly said, "You might need these tonight." He'd noticed I forgot them on the bus and grabbed them for me. Thank God for Clarence! He handed me my cleats and we both smiled. Then he said, "One more thing . . . go out and enjoy it tonight. I'm behind you. I know you'll do great."

At the time, I didn't realize how big that moment was. But the more I think about it now, the more I understand how meaningful the brief exchange with Clarence was. It made a huge difference in my mentality that night. Leading up to that moment, I had been nervous, but right after that, for some reason all the nerves went away.

I can't thank Clarence enough for what he did for me that night. He saved me. He probably never thinks about that moment, but I do all the time. Not only was he looking out for me and my cleats, but he also had the character to say those words to me. Once I knew Clarence believed in me and wished me well, I knew the rest of the team felt the same way. It gave me a ton of confidence.

The most amazing thing about this story is the fact that Clarence was the guy I was replacing that night. Here he was, a guy who got injured the day before this huge game, looking out for a younger, inexperienced player who was getting an opportunity in his place. It would have been so easy for him

to be down about his injury and to be bitter, and for him to turn his shoulder away from me in that moment. But he didn't. In fact, he did just the opposite and went out of his way to help me. I will forever have the utmost respect for Clarence as a person and player because of what he did for me that day.

Who knows what would have happened if I didn't have my cleats that night. Maybe I would have had to play in another teammate's cleats that were a size too big or too small. Maybe I would have had to play in my socks. (Just kidding.) What I do know is that I got to play, in my own cleats, thanks to Clarence. And our team played one of its best games ever against Mexico.

Thank you, Clarence, for remembering my cleats on the bus. Thank you for looking out for me and giving me confidence. You taught me a lot that night about how to be a good teammate.

LEARNING
THE HARD WAY

Lesson of the day: Do NOT play truth or dare on the bench during a game.

Early in my second year as a professional, we were playing at Seattle. I wasn't getting much playing time so far that season and I wasn't sure if I would be included on the trip. However, I had a strong week of practice and made the traveling squad. Only eighteen players suit up for a game. The "traveling eighteen" list is posted in alphabetical order, so my name was toward the top. I quickly looked down the list to see if my teammate, roommate, and fellow second-year player, Graham Zusi, was on it. His name was, too! I remember being excited to make the traveling squad because Seattle has one of the best playing atmospheres in the entire league. Also, I knew there was only a small chance I would be playing, so there was no real pressure. I was going to get to travel to Seattle, have some fun, and cheer on my teammates from the bench.

That season, we used to play a game that was sort of like truth or dare, but without the truths. (So maybe it should have just been called "dare," but we never really gave it an official name.) Basically, when someone called you out to do something, you had to step up and accept it, or back down and decline it. But on a team of alpha males trying to outcompete each other, it was pretty rare that someone declined a dare.

We left for Seattle on Friday, one day before our match on Saturday evening. Travel days were always a prime time for this made-up game. Public places, such as airports, added an extra bit of adrenaline to a dare. Also, because it was the day before a game, everyone's mood was still light and most guys enjoyed joking around. On this particular trip, there had already been a bunch of accepted dares. One guy had walked through the terminal with his shirt off, and another had eaten a handful of jalapeños at lunch.

As an unwritten rule, we never played the dare game on game day. On game day, we were serious and focused all our energy on preparing to win. It wasn't that we tightened up—we still joked around at times. It's just that we didn't egg each other on with dares like a normal day. When I woke up on that game day, I remember being excited and nervous. Although it was unlikely I would play one minute, I still had game day butterflies. I told myself I was going to prepare like I was playing, just in case my number was called. I hydrated, took a nap, stretched, and ate like I was going to play. I listened to the songs I normally listened to before I play. In warm-ups, I prepared my body like I was going to play. I went through my mental checklist and visualized as if I was going to play.

I was locked into the game mentally, but trust me, it's a different feeling when you know you're going to play than when you know you're not. As the kickoff whistle sounded, I loosened up my shoes, took off my shin guards, and got comfortable to watch my teammates. Subs usually don't start warming up until the second half, so I had a good forty-five to sixty minutes before I had to do anything. I remember being excited to watch the game from the bench . . . 50,000 fans, on the road, two good teams. Doesn't get much better.

Around the fifteen-minute mark, I reached down by the bench and picked up a Gatorade bottle, fruit punch flavor to be exact. Just as I opened it to take a small sip, Graham Zusi, who was sitting next to me, said, "I dare you to chug it!" I said, "The whole thing?" "Yeah, the whole thing! You won't do it," he responded. Our exchange caught the attention of the rest of the bench . . . and they were all looking at me. Just like that, it was on. I had a decision to make. Actually it wasn't that much of a decision. Like I said, I wasn't really planning on going into the game. Plus, it really wasn't that big of a challenge. Chugging a bottle of Gatorade? I had been challenged to way harder dares than that.

"Winning means you're willing to go longer, work harder, and give more than anyone else."

—Vince Lombardi

This was cake. So I stepped up, accepted the dare, and chugged the entire bottle in under five seconds. I think everyone on the bench got a good laugh out of it.

Literally thirty seconds after I finished chugging, Jimmy Conrad, our captain and starting central defender, went down with a calf strain. I remember seeing this and panicking because I knew I was Jimmy's back-up at the time. Here I was, a young second-year player, about to go into a game in front of 50,000 people. Without a warm-up and having just chugged an entire bottle of Gatorade as a joke!

I remember scrambling to find my shin guards and tie my cleats. Head coach Peter Vermes was yelling at me to hurry up because I had to get onto the field immediately. So there I went, entering the match as an unprepared substitute early in the first half.

I knew I had to be smart about easing my way into the game because I wasn't properly warmed up. Unfortunately, it didn't quite work out that way. As soon as I entered the match, Seattle started putting the pressure on us by hitting ball after ball behind our back line. I made about fifty sprints in those first five minutes on the field. (OK, it was probably more like ten, but it seemed like fifty.)

Surprisingly, my muscles warmed up quicker than I thought. But that wasn't the issue—my stomach was. After playing for five minutes, I got the worst side cramp I'd ever had in my life. I could barely even run, all because of that stupid Gatorade! I'm telling you, it was painful. Usually side cramps are just annoying. They stick around for a few minutes and fade out, but not this one. This one stayed with me for the entire first half. To this day, it was probably the longest thirty-minute period of soccer I've ever had to play. I was holding on for dear life in front of 50,000 people, trying not to puke. I knew if I puked, I would never hear the end of it. I remember looking over at the bench and seeing the look on my teammates' faces. I could tell they all felt bad. I made eye contact with Graham and with his eyes he said, "Oops, sorry, dude."

Somehow, I made it into halftime and regrouped. Eventually, my side cramp faded and I settled into the game. I ended up putting in a decent performance, though we lost the game on a questionable last-minute goal.

A few years later, Graham and I were both on the bench for a World Cup qualifying match with the U.S. Men's National Team. In the first half, I saw him reach down and pick up a Gatorade. Of course, I called him out—I couldn't resist! But all we did was laugh. We had both learned our lesson in Seattle . . . never chug a Gatorade right before you're about to go in. Or even better, never play dare on the bench during a game!

GATORADE

A VIEW FROM
THE BACKFIELD

The view from the backfield isn't always pretty. In my opinion, being a defender is the hardest position in soccer. I can already hear the groans coming from players at all the other positions, but hey, it's my book, so I'll make my case. . . .

As a defender, your main job is to prevent the other team from scoring. When you don't, it's your fault. If that sounds brutal . . . well, it is.

I can trace my stance on this directly to Peter Vermes (along with a few of my other coaches, especially Bobby Clark, my head coach at Notre Dame). Peter has always preached the importance of defense and puts pressure on his defenders to carry a ton of responsibility. Not surprisingly, it's where we put the most emphasis in training and games.

Whenever our team gets together to watch film, we focus on how we can defend better as a team. Many times when a mistake happens higher up the field, we trace it back to the defenders and then discuss ways we could have prevented it. Because I've been playing for Peter for almost eight years now, I've adopted this same mentality. Whenever something goes wrong, I look at myself first and then the rest of the defenders to figure out something we could have done better.

There's almost *always* something you could have done to prevent a goal. Sometimes it's your physical actions that lead to a goal; sometimes it's your mental decisions. Even when it seems like someone else is obviously to blame—like when a goalie completely messes up and allows a ball to go through his hands—it feels like it's still your fault.

Why? Because when you look at every goal scored, you can *always* go back and find a moment when a defender could have done something differently. Sometimes you only need to rewind a few seconds. Other times it was something you could have done differently earlier in the game that would have prevented the goal. But every single action and decision you make has an impact on the play.

For example, that play when the goalie completely messed up and let the ball go through his hands? What were you doing on that play? Were you close to the ball? Could you have blocked the shot from even happening?

Not surprisingly, this is one of my least favorite parts about being a defender—the belief that every time the other team scores a goal, I could have done something to stop it. After a game, I will replay a goal hundreds of times in my head. If only I had done this or that. . . .

Here's my (partial) list of reasons why my team might give up a goal:

I DIDN'T BLOCK A SHOT.
I DIDN'T STAY WITH MY MAN.
I DIDN'T CLEAR THE BALL
    WELL ENOUGH.
I DIDN'T JUMP HIGH ENOUGH
    TO WIN THE HEADER.
I MISREAD THE BOUNCE
    OF THE BALL.
I MISREAD THE SPIN
    OF THE BALL.
I DIDN'T STEP UP FAST ENOUGH.
I KEPT A PLAYER ONSIDE.
I FOULED A GUY IN THE BOX.
I COMMITTED A HANDBALL
    IN THE BOX.
I STEPPED TOO HIGH AND THEY
    PLAYED IT OVER MY HEAD.
I DIDN'T COVER FOR ONE
    OF MY TEAMMATES.
I DIDN'T COMMUNICATE.
I DIDN'T ORGANIZE.

Notice what all these reasons have in common? Yep, they all start with "I." Welcome to the mind-set of a defender. (Trust me—it's no place you want to be after a loss.) Seriously, I could look at almost every goal any of my teams has ever given up, and I could tell you something I would and should have done differently. Does this seem like a lot of responsibility? It is. There's a lot of weight on your shoulders . . . and that's one of the reasons why being a defender is the hardest position.

As a defender, you're not only judged by how many good plays you make, but also by how many mistakes you make. A typical comment about a good defender is something like this: "That player al-ways seems to be in the right spot at the right time, and almost never makes a mistake."

But we all make mistakes. It's impossible not to. The key, of course, is to limit your mistakes as much as possible and to learn from them. And when you do make one, hope it's not a big one. Little mistakes might affect a possession and cause a turnover. Big mistakes change the outcome of a game. Big mistakes can cost the team a championship and ultimately hurt your career.

I can't tell you how many times I've played a good game but afterward only thought about the few mistakes I made. No matter what I tell myself, I can't get them out of my head.

"The great part about playing soccer is there's always the next game. There's always another opportunity to correct a mistake you've made. The key to getting better as a defender is LEARNING from a mistake and putting in the work to make sure it doesn't happen again."

IT'S ONLY A MISTAKE IF YOU DON'T LEARN FROM IT

In September 2014, we played the New York Red Bulls and I got called for a foul inside my own box early in the first half. I made a mistake. I mistimed a slide tackle trying to block a shot at the last second and caught Bradley Wright-Phillips on the foot, causing him to fall down. The referee blew the whistle, pointed to the spot, and Bradley Wright-Phillips converted the penalty kick to put his team up 1–0. Of course we still had the rest of the game to mount a comeback, but unfortunately we weren't able to and the Red Bulls went on to win 2–1.

It was a tough loss to deal with. I knew the entire team, myself included, had put a tremendous amount of effort into the game, and I felt like we lost because of my penalty. Immediately after the game, I struggled to get my mind off the mistake. Twitter was not a friendly place. It was hard to sleep that night because I kept replaying the mistake in my head. I eventually turned on the TV around 3:00 a.m. hoping to find a random movie such as *The Dark Knight* or *Wedding Crashers,* and of course . . . the local station was replaying the game! To make it worse, I started watching right before I made my mistake, so I had to see it again. I can't make this stuff up.

The next morning, I still felt like it was all my fault. I remember feeling embarrassed when I got on the team bus in Hoboken, New Jersey, to fly back home. Somewhere along the way to Newark Airport, a voice in my head told me I had to stop beating myself up about the mistake I made. I couldn't let it bring me down any longer. In that moment, I stopped worrying and decided I was going to get something out of the situation.

The next day (our off day) I went into the training facility to watch the film of the play I made. I watched it over and over again with the coaching staff. After much discussion, I knew exactly what I would do differently next time. Instead of slide tackling and giving my opponent an easy penalty kick, I would stay on my feet and force my opponent to make a more difficult shot. I couldn't wait to get back onto the field and play another game.

That week in practice, I emphasized what I learned.

A few weeks later, I was put in a similar situation at home against the Chicago Fire. It was late in the game and we were leading 1–0. Quincy Amarikwa had a chance in front of goal. He had a step on me, but instead of sliding and potentially fouling him like I did against New York, I stayed patient and forced him into a difficult angle shot that our goalkeeper easily saved. We went on to win the game 2–0.

I'm not saying that decision was the reason we won the game, but if I had tried to slide tackle in the box again, who knows what would have happened? Maybe I would have mistimed my challenge again and the referee would have called a penalty kick. That didn't happen because I forced myself to learn from my mistake earlier in the season.

When you make a mistake, try not to focus on the mistake itself. Don't let the mistake work against you—make it work for you. Making a mistake is an opportunity to get stronger. There's a quote I love: "Be like the grass . . . the more crap they throw on you, the stronger you get!"

When you're a defender, you're not remembered for the good plays you make, but the bad ones. The hard truth is that, as a defender, you typically don't have much chance of being the hero, but you have a great shot at being the goat!

In my opinion, the opposite is true for attacking players. Because they're positioned up the field, they have the luxury of making mistakes without too many consequences. Actually, they're encouraged to make mistakes. It proves they're "being creative" and "taking risks." If a forward misses nine shots in a game, it might not matter because one goal changes everything. Ah, the glorious life of an attacking player!

NO PLACE FOR THE MEEK: INSIDE THE MIND OF A DEFENDER

Things I think about during a game:

- Make sure your partner at center back is on the exact same line as you.
- Every single time the other team plays the ball backward, step our line up and steal space.
- Don't let the other team play the ball behind you.
- When the other team has a throw-in, make sure everyone has a man marked tightly—no easy throw-ins!
- When we have a goal kick, open up as quickly as possible to create an angle so the goalkeeper can play you the ball.
- When the other team has a goal kick, make sure everyone in front of you turns around immediately and prevents the other team from playing.
- When the other team has a free kick, make sure someone gets in front of the ball so the other team can't play quick.
- Don't allow the forward to receive the ball and turn—always make him play backward!
- When the ball gets switched, release your outside back as soon as you get in a position to help.
- If there's about to be a cross, find your man and lock into him.
- When the ball is on one side of the field, open your shoulders so you can see what's going on behind you.
- When one of the other defenders goes up for a header, make sure to cover behind him five to ten yards in case he doesn't win it.
- Tell the midfielders in front of you to move right or left so they cut out any passes played on the ground.

> **"The only thing that was missing initially with Matt was the fact that he was too quiet. Central defenders need to be leaders, and Matt was quiet. He led by example but needed to be more vocal with the players around him. He grew into this, and it is good to watch him play at the very highest level taking charge."**
>
> —Bobby Clark, Notre Dame men's soccer coach

- If the other team is running at you with the ball, drop and delay!
- Organize everyone on set pieces.

How do you accomplish all these? One answer: **COMMUNICATION.** You have to constantly talk throughout the game. In every moment, there's a decision to make and instructions to give. Talk to your teammates. Give them information. If you don't, you're making life extremely difficult for yourself.

After a game, you should be physically tired *and* mentally tired. Peter Vermes has always told me that I've done a good job if after a game my mind is exhausted and I can barely speak because I've lost my voice. That's a sign you've been thinking and communicating the entire match.

Playing this way takes a pretty extraordinary level of fitness, but not necessarily the kind you're probably thinking about. Being physically fit is one thing. Being mentally fit is another. People think if you're able to run around the entire game without getting tired, you're fit. That's true in a sense, but that's not good enough, especially as a central defender. You have to be able to run around while also talking the entire game. This adds a completely different dynamic. It's something you have to train your body to do. Talking loudly and clearly takes a lot of energy. Think about how loud stadiums get. To be heard, you have to scream

as loud as possible. Think about running around for ninety minutes and screaming at the top of your lungs—all at the same time! It's a lot harder than people imagine. Next time you go out for a run or workout, try it. (Just be warned that people might look at you rather strangely and will probably cross to the other side of the street.)

It's one of the biggest challenges I have throughout the game. When I get tired (everyone does), my breathing becomes heavy, which makes it difficult to communicate. You're absolutely sucking wind trying to talk but nothing is coming out because you can't get enough oxygen to your lungs. It's not a great feeling!

The Constant Fight

INJURIES, BENCHINGS, AND A BUNCH OF OTHER STUFF THAT STINKS BUT YOU'D BETTER LEARN TO DEAL WITH

"Adversity creates opportunity. When obstacles are placed in front of you, don't say 'Why me?' Instead say 'How can I overcome this?'"

—MB 5

HOW TO SIT
ON A BENCH

First things first—being on the bench isn't fun. No one really likes it. I think we all can agree that everyone wants to be on the field playing. In a perfect world, none of us would ever have to sit on the bench.

Unfortunately we don't live in a perfect world. There *always* has to be someone sitting on the bench and *you* will have to be one of those people at some point. That's right, no matter who you are, how old you are, or how good you are, you

What can I do to still make a positive difference?
How can this make me better?

THE BENCH

will end up sitting on the bench at some point in your life. I know some of you may think it won't happen to you . . . you're THAT good. But it will, I promise. At some point in their lives, Michael Jordan, LeBron James, Steph Curry, Lionel Messi, Abby Wambach, Cristiano Ronaldo, Tom Brady—all of them had to sit on the bench . . . and so will you.

So if sitting on the bench is inevitable, wouldn't it be smart to think about how to handle it? Shouldn't you prepare for this situation?

Unfortunately, I don't think many of us give much, if any, thought to playing a role on the bench. It goes against human nature. Our plan is to play, not to sit on the bench, so why would we need to prepare for something we don't plan on doing? The answer is because it's very important. It can be argued that being prepared for a bench role is just as important as being prepared for a playing role. That's because the bench role is a lot harder and will challenge you in more ways than playing on the field. Your character, unselfishness, strength, and mental fortitude will all be tested in ways you will never be able to duplicate on the field.

When your moment comes, your "turn" to sit on the bench, you have to be ready for it. It won't be easy. In fact, you'll probably struggle with it. That's OK. Most people do. Most people will lose a bit of confidence and let it affect their mood. Most people will be frustrated and angry at the world. But if you view it as a challenge, then you and everyone else will find out what you're truly made of. It will be hard to stay positive and focused on doing your job. However, if you can dig deep and still find a way to do all the small things right—work hard, show up on time, participate, prepare your teammates, have a good attitude—you'll make an enormous statement to yourself and to everyone around you.

I've had to sit on the bench many times before, for many different reasons. One time early in my career, I was on the bench behind an older, more experienced player. Of course, I believed I was better than this player and deserved to be playing. (Everyone thinks this.) I pouted for a few days and felt sorry for myself. I felt the coach was being stupid. During the games while I sat on the bench watching my teammates, a small part of me felt the urge to root against the older player. Maybe if he messed up, it would give me the chance to play. Luckily, I quickly realized this is NEVER the right mentality to have. If you're ever feeling this same urge (I know a lot of people do), please catch yourself in the act and STOP. You will not be rewarded for having this mentality. It's not the right way to handle the situation.

From my experience, one of the easiest things to see is if a teammate wants you and the team to do well. If you're bitter, there's no way to hide it. You will be found out very quickly. Conversely, if you're supportive, you'll instantly gain respect from your team.

At another point—this time later in my career—I had to sit on the bench for a few weeks in the middle of the season. Again, it was hard not to put my head down at the

---

"Everyone goes through adversity in life, but what matters is how you learn from it."

**—Lou Holtz, former Notre Dame
head football coach**

The best way to handle this situation is to be genuinely supportive of your teammates. Remember, no one is ever bigger than the team, and your individual success will always come from team success. Ask yourself this question: When you finally get a chance to be on the field, do you want a bunch of your teammates over on the bench hoping *you* screw up? Or would you rather have them cheering you on?

time. It was frustrating and difficult to stay positive. It was also difficult to put the same energy and focus into each practice as I had when I was playing. When practice started or a drill began, I had the tendency to ask myself, "What's the point? It's not like how I do will matter because I'm going to be on the bench." I was wrong. Despite not having a direct impact on the field, I still could have a major impact on my team's success. I challenged

"Remember, just because you start doesn't make you better than your teammates who don't. Just because the coach looks to you when the game is on the line doesn't make you a winner. A winner is someone who handles adversity with grace and dignity. A winner is someone who is willing to sacrifice his needs for the team's greater good. There are many starters who would immediately crack if they were subjected to having to sit on the bench the way the reserves have to do game in, game out."

—Dr. Alan Goldberg, author of thirty-five
sports performance books

myself to make an impact in other ways. Control what you can control! If you can't control the decision to be playing or not (usually the coach controls that), find something you can control. Make sure everyone is mentally prepared for the game. Give your teammates confidence before the game. Make sure you're mentally and physically ready, too, just in case you get called upon. There are many ways to make an impact from the sideline . . . find yours and go for it.

Back to when I wasn't playing . . . I remember doing a drill midweek that was helping our team get ready for the weekend's game. It was clear I wouldn't be in the starting lineup and the drill we were doing focused on the starters. They would get five or six reps and then the reserve players would get one or two reps. So it was hard to get into a rhythm. I got frustrated that I wasn't as involved, especially since I was so used to getting the majority of the reps. For a minute or two, I shrugged my shoulders and gritted my teeth in anger.

Then I looked over my shoulder and noticed there were two young academy players practicing with us that day—and it hit me. What impression was I going to leave with those kids? What example was I going to set for them? I guarantee they were excited to be practicing with the first team that morning. Wouldn't it be a shame if I ruined their experience because I was angry from not playing? Wouldn't it be a shame if they walked away saying, "Matt Besler has a bad attitude"? I quickly changed my mentality. For the rest of the session, I was locked in. I was encouraging, positive, and loud, and I worked my tail off. I have no idea if I made an impact on either of those kids. I'm sure they didn't notice, but perhaps they did. Maybe one day those kids will be in the same situation and they'll think back to that day and remember how I didn't pout and how I handled it. All I know is I walked off the practice field that day with my head held high (even when I knew I wouldn't play that weekend) because I knew I put everything I had into helping our team prepare and I knew I got everything I could out of practice. It felt good.

Bottom line: You're going to face a situation like this at some point. Everyone will. It's part of life. And the only thing you have complete control over is how you handle it. How will you respond? You can choose to handle the situation with class, character, and graciousness. Or you can pout, give up, and bring your team down with you. The choice is yours.

FAIL!
NOW WHAT?

Failure is scary. Not many people talk about failure, and those who do typically don't enjoy it. It's hard to be open and honest when it comes to failure.

I've seen failure bring down a lot of people, me included. One of the problems we have when dealing with failure is the way we perceive it. Our perception of failure is often this big, dark, scary monster that no one wants to face. We've let the perception of failure grow into something really intimidating. Maybe we do it ourselves, maybe society does it, or maybe it's a mixture of both.

Whatever the case, being intimidated and scared is the wrong perception to have of failure. We must change our mentality. Failure isn't some scary, dark, mysterious thing. Failure is everywhere. Failure is inevitable.

Failure is common. We have to accept this fact and not be afraid. It's the only chance we have if we want to deal with failure in a positive way.

If we all agree that failure is bound to happen, we should stop trying to control it. It's impossible anyway. Failure will happen to you. It happens to everyone. The question isn't IF, but WHEN failure will happen to you. You have to be ready for failure. And because you can't control it, you must focus on something you can control. So when you fail, how will you deal with it?

There are basically two responses to failure:

1. I will handle failure negatively.

2. I will handle failure positively.

This is a big decision. Notice I said "decision." You have a CHOICE about how you respond. Please, choose the second response. It's your only chance to grow as a person or a player.

The next time you fail at something, I challenge you to follow these steps:

1. Accept that you've failed.

2. Take a deep breath. Realize it's OK and that it happens to everyone.

3. Choose to respond positively.

4. Look forward. Focus on something you can take away from the experience.

HEAD AND HEART: MY CONCUSSION STORY

I was first introduced to the word "concussion" in 1995 when I was in second grade. My teammate and childhood friend Ryan Copp was playing soccer and took a vicious clearance directly off his forehead. He came out of the game and we learned later that he had a concussion. I certainly didn't understand the clinical details at the time. All I knew was that a concussion was a head injury.

Ten years later, I became more personally familiar with the word. My younger brother Mike was the quarterback for his high school football team and took some big helmet-to-helmet hits, causing him to miss a few days of school when he experienced headaches and drowsiness. I was a freshman in college at the time, and even though Mike's experience taught me a little more about the physical effects of a concussion, I was still extremely naive.

It wasn't until I became a professional that I realized the devastating impact a concussion—or a series of concussions—could have. In 2011, I witnessed the cumulative effect of concussions end the career of one of my most respected teammates, Jimmy Conrad. Jimmy was about eight years older than me, and I looked up to him in many ways. At the time, he had accomplished most of the things I was working toward and he taught me a lot about being a professional. Unfortunately, Jimmy suffered multiple concussions throughout his playing career, especially toward the end, which ultimately forced him to retire.

By witnessing Jimmy's battle with concussion damage, I learned many things:

- Once you've had one concussion, you're more likely to have another.
- Your next concussion is always the most dangerous.
- Damage caused by concussions can be severe enough to not only end your career, but to permanently affect your life outside of sports.

Because I witnessed Jimmy's experience up close, I felt like I had a decent grasp on the issue. A concussion was a serious matter and it needed to be treated that way.

Still, I never thought it would happen to me. And other than feeling pain and sympathy when others suffered them, I didn't give concussions a whole lot of thought. That all changed on March 24, 2016.

INJURY

I was in Guatemala City with the U.S. Men's National Team for a World Cup qualifying match against Guatemala. The night before the match, we had our official training in the stadium. It was our standard "match day minus one" practice, a routine practice we had done many times before.

With about five minutes left, we were playing a small-sided game. My team was defending when a ball popped out to Michael Bradley at the top of our box. He took one touch to set himself up, and fired a shot back toward our goal. I was standing in front of our goal, directly in the path of Michael's shot and had no time to react. I remember instinctively ducking my head slightly right before the ball struck me. I tensed up my shoulders and neck, and the ball hit me square in the center of my head. It knocked me off balance, but I didn't experience any immediate pain. To be honest, I had been hit harder before.

My teammates took a few seconds to make sure I was OK, and then we resumed practice. I was actually pumped because I'd made a strong defensive play and saved my team a goal. I even remember my team's goalkeeper, who was behind me, yelling, "Great job, Matty!" As a defender, you're taught to sacrifice your body in order to block a shot, and that's exactly what I'd done.

A few minutes later, coach blew the whistle and instructed everyone to take five minutes on our own. This meant we could do whatever extra work we wanted.

I joined up with a couple other defenders and we started hitting some longer balls over distance, to get used to the field and how it bounced. I'd felt fine up till then, but when I broadened my field of vision to include the stadium lights, my vision began to blur. The lights seemed brighter than normal, and I had a hard time tracking the ball in the air. When I received a ball, I felt like my touch was off. In controlling and passing, I couldn't feel the ball like I normally did. It almost felt like an out-of-body experience, like I was in a dream.

Still, because I wasn't running around and physically putting stress on my body, I figured I was safe to continue passing with my teammates for the last few minutes of practice. However, the lightheadedness and blurry vision got worse, so I went up to our trainers and told them exactly how I was feeling. I told them about the lights and about the trouble I had simply passing the ball. They administered a few quick memory tests right there on the field. I remembered what day it was, my birth date, where I was, how the play happened—all good signs for ruling out a concussion. Also,

I didn't have a headache, another good sign. We decided to head back to the hotel where they would closely monitor me for the rest of the night.

We got back to the hotel an hour later and ate dinner together as a team. I actually started feeling better. I think getting some food in my stomach helped. My blurry vision and lightheadedness improved. Again, I checked in with the trainers to run some tests, and most everything appeared to be fine. We agreed that after a good night's sleep, everything would more than likely feel back to normal. This meant I would be good to go for the game the next day. I remember feeling confident as I left the training room.

I went upstairs and got into bed, looking forward to sleeping off the symptoms I experienced earlier that night.

But within five minutes of my head hitting the pillow, I knew it wasn't over. I felt a sharp pain in the side of my head and intense pain in my eyelids, right beneath my eyebrows. I typically don't get headaches, so I didn't realize what was happening. I tried to relax and switch positions but it had no effect. I put a pillow over my head hoping to relieve the pressure, but that didn't help either. After about an hour of struggling though the pain, I realized I wasn't going to be able to get through it on my own. I at least needed some Advil. I called our trainer, just as he had instructed me to do if anything didn't feel right, and he told me to meet him down in his room in ten minutes.

As I walked down to his room, the symptoms intensified. The motion made my head pound, and I was getting nauseous. I had to keep one eye open and one eye closed just to make it down the hall. Once I made it to the training room, I lay down and tried to stay calm. Since Advil or Tylenol might mask the symptoms of a concussion, we decided I shouldn't take anything. I then took the official sport concussion assessment tool test, which lasted about twenty minutes. I'm not sure how I scored, but I was mentally stable enough to remember everything going on. Another ten minutes passed and the symptoms kept getting worse, causing me to vomit. At that point, our trainer and doctor decided to take me to the hospital for a computerized tomography (CT) scan to make sure there wasn't any bleeding in the brain.

I honestly don't remember how I got from the hotel to the hospital. I have one small mental snapshot of riding in the back of a car with the window open as it moved through the city streets, but that's it. All I remember is "waking up" in a hospital bed with a bright light shining on me. It felt like I was awakening from surgery. I looked to the side and saw our trainer, doctor, and head of team security. They informed me of the plan—get a CT scan and have a neurosurgeon come in and read the report. I got the scan and waited for the doctor to arrive.

The waiting didn't help the situation. All it did was give me time to worry. I was legitimately scared in that moment. Forget soccer, forget everything else . . . I thought my life was in danger. I feared there might be irreversible damage. I was anxious almost to the point of panicking, because I was no longer in control of my brain, which meant I wasn't in control of my body either. I remember sitting there, feeling alone and desperate, trying to make a deal with God: "God, please listen to me. I know I've asked for a lot in my life, and You've already given me so much . . . but I really need You right now. Please, somehow get me out of this situation. If You do, I promise I will thank You every day for the rest of my life."

So there I sat, waiting and going back and forth between desperation, fear, and faith.

Unfortunately, the timing of the injury was a major obstacle. When I was admitted to the hospital, it was 11:15 p.m. on Thursday during Holy Week. Most of Guatemala—a predominantly Catholic country—was on holiday. The hospital was empty. A nurse told us the entire country shuts down over Holy Week, especially starting on Good Friday through Easter Sunday. At one point

"The mark of great sportsmen is not how good they are at their best, but how good they are at their worst."

—Martina Navratilova, nine-time Wimbledon champion

In the meantime, I got hooked up to an IV, which immediately helped with the nausea. I could feel the medicine travel through my bloodstream, giving my entire body a calming sensation. For the first time in two hours, I felt like I wasn't going to throw up. I started to feel relaxed. Next, a shot in my right gluteus stung at first but caused my headache to ease almost immediately. It was amazing. The ringing and pounding stopped. My mind finally started to feel clear.

I asked our trainer what time it was. He told me 12:15 a.m.—so it was officially Good Friday. Great. Here I was, sitting in a hospital bed in the middle of Guatemala where almost nobody was working because of a national holiday. It didn't give me a whole lot of comfort.

I was also concerned because I was a U.S. soccer player. The U.S. State Department lists the threat of violent crime in Guatemala as "critical," and the number of violent crimes against U.S. citizens and other foreigners is high. Everyone in the country knew the game was the following day. It was the biggest game for Guatemala in a long time, maybe ever. If word got out that one of the U.S. players was staying at the hospital, who knows what would happen. I already felt like I was in a hostile environment, but this added another degree of fear and anxiety. Fortunately, our head of security and his team knew exactly what precautions to take. They even arranged for some Secret Service agents from the U.S. Embassy to be stationed at the hospital. I felt like I was in some kind of movie—like I was stranded in this empty hospital in the middle of Guatemala, with Secret Service agents protecting me from soccer hooligans trying to break into the hospital and kidnap me! I'm sure I was letting my mind get a little too worked up. Nonetheless, I did feel a lot safer once the agents showed up.

The doctor finally arrived around 2:00 a.m. Later, we learned he was the only neurosurgeon in the city and he was on vacation at the beach with his family when my injury occurred. Looking back, I can't thank him enough for taking time out of his vacation to come back to the city to help out some random American in the middle of the night.

Our interactions didn't start very well though. When he came into my room after reading the CT scan, the first thing he said, in broken English, was, "This is worse than I thought." I started freaking out. Honestly, I started preparing myself for the worst. I pictured myself going in for brain surgery or something like that. Again, I feared for my life.

Our head of security, Johnny, is fluent in Spanish, so he asked the doctor to clarify. They spoke in Spanish for about a minute—a very long minute—before Johnny explained everything to me. Fortunately, the doctor's initial comment had been a bit lost in translation. He had been told over the phone on his way in that some soccer player got bumped on the head and had a headache. So when he arrived, heard what happened, and saw me puking and hooked up to the IV, he meant that the symptoms were worse than he expected. The doctor informed us that the CT scan looked good—no bleeding. And no brain surgery! This was the best news possible. Still, the doctor wanted me to stay overnight at the hospital for observation. I nodded my head to the doctor and said, "Muchas gracias." Also, I asked Johnny to tell him that while I appreciated his attempt to speak English to me, I'd rather have him speak Spanish and have Johnny translate to avoid any more misinterpretations. That strategy worked much better.

I spent the rest of the morning in a hospital room resting while being monitored. I took a step back from all that happened and tried to make sense of the situation. I also took the opportunity to call my wife, Amanda.

While in Guatemala we'd had very limited phone access. Amanda wasn't aware that I had hit my head the evening before at practice, so needless to say it was a shock when she answered my call that morning and I told her I was lying in a hospital bed. I quickly filled her in while leaving out the details that might have worried her even more. I basically tried to comfort her as much as possible. I told her that I was fine and everything was going to be all right. It's hard to imagine what it would be like to get a call from your spouse from a hospital in a foreign country, and

there's nothing you can do to help the situation. That's exactly why I didn't call her earlier. I knew there was nothing she could do, and calling her would only make things worse. She would have been stuck at home in Kansas City worrying all night. All the same, I did feel somewhat guilty for waiting to tell her. Before the call ended, I asked Amanda to call the rest of my family and fill them in. I didn't want them freaking out later that night when they sat down to watch the game and found out I wasn't playing because of a head injury.

After the phone call, I had about four hours until I could be discharged. That meant more time to wait, which meant more time to think. Again, my mind started racing out of control with fear and desperation. I no longer feared for my life, but I feared for my career. I knew I had just suffered a serious concussion. Am I ever going to play again? Will I have to retire? What am I going to do with my life? For the first time ever, I questioned whether or not it was even *worth* playing. It was a scary, lonely place to be. Again, I talked with God: "God, please help me again. Just get me out of here.

Get me back home to my wife and family. Nothing else matters in this moment. If I have to give up soccer in order to be healthy and safe again, I'm willing. I promise if You get me home and make me better, I will never forget this prayer."

After another hour of playing mental games with myself, I finally dozed off. Three hours later, it was time to leave the hospital and return to the team hotel. Physically, I felt good. The headache and nausea were both gone. All that remained was a feeling of drowsiness and lightheadedness. I also felt a bit clumsy, like I wasn't fully in control of my motor functions. The plan for me once I got back to the hotel was to lay low while the training staff continued to monitor me. It wasn't safe for me to fly yet, so I knew I would be spending a few more days in Guatemala before going home.

RECOVERY

If the difficulty of the injury was a seven on a scale of one to ten, the recovery process was a nine. The injury itself was a short, intense panic. The recovery process was a drawn-out exercise in frustration and anxiety.

One thing that gave me hope during this period was hearing from other people who had suffered concussions. They assured me things would eventually get back to normal. They said that all of a sudden everything would clear up and—just like that—I would feel better. The difficult part was waiting for that moment, and there was nothing I could do to control it. I would go to bed at night thinking and praying that the next morning would finally be the day everything would clear up. I'd fall asleep full of hope and confidence. In the morning, all of that would go away as soon as I got out of bed, went to the bathroom, and realized nothing had changed. I still had symptoms. Still felt messed up. Some mornings, my confidence would last a little longer, maybe an hour or so, until I got into my car and started driving to practice. Sooner or later, though, the symptoms would reappear, and I was left to hope the next day would be the day I felt better. This cycle lasted about three weeks.

The recovery process was so frustrating because there were so few clear answers. My first question when I returned home was "How long will I be out?" The response: "We don't know." My second question was "What can I do for treatment?" Same response: "We don't know." And when you're actually given an answer, it's a gray answer, not black and white. Professional athletes hate gray answers. When an injury happens, we are trained to face it head on. First question after an ankle sprain: "How long until I'm back?" Next question: "What can I do for treatment?" And you're given an answer. You're told how long you can expect to be out. Sprained ankle: three to six weeks. Broken bone: six to eight weeks. Muscle strain: two to three months. You get a timetable. You can set a goal and compete with yourself on making it back. It gives you purpose and a finish line. With a concussion, doctors and trainers can't really give you an accurate timetable. It's impossible to estimate. Each person is different. Each head injury is different.

Also, for a nonhead injury, doctors can give you a bunch of treatments and exercises that will help you recover, such as ice, stimulation, stretching, and compression. This is great for an athlete because it makes you feel like you're actually doing something to help. But for a concussion, there's not a whole lot you can do other than let it recover on its own, which makes you feel helpless.

I was happy to learn about some recent advancements in the treatment for concussions. One treatment designed to accelerate recovery is called vestibular rehab. This entails exercises such as sitting on a chair and focusing on a point across the room while moving your head side to side, or holding your finger out in front of your face and moving it diagonally across your visual field. One exercise that seemed to help me a lot required me to pick out a few objects in the room and move from one to the next while focusing as fast as I could. At first, this made me dizzy and it took at least a few seconds to focus on each object. But after a week or so, I got better.

Eventually, I felt symptom-free throughout the day. I woke up without feeling lightheaded. I could drive without getting dizzy. I started regaining my coordination when I went on walks with my family. Once I reached that point, it was time to start the physical aspect of the recovery process.

My first day, I began by riding a stationary bike for twenty minutes. I didn't have any recurring symptoms. The next day I moved up to thirty minutes, then forty minutes. Again, no recurring symptoms. I then progressed to the elliptical machine, which proved a bit more challenging than the stationary bike. I completed a few workouts on this machine without experiencing symptoms, which meant it was time to start jogging. With jogging, I started on the treadmill before going outside on the field. It was important to control the environment at first, and being inside on a treadmill kept outside stimulation to a minimum. After a few days jogging on the treadmill, I was cleared to go outside and start running on the field. (It's important to mention that I progressed through these stages without any setbacks. However, if I had experienced symptoms again at any moment, I would have had to stop and move back a stage until I could get through the exercise without any symptoms.)

I hit my first physical recovery hurdle when I started outdoor running. My vision felt very unstable. Normally when you run, as you move up and down and side to side, your visual field remains stable, allowing you to focus on what you're seeing. When I first started running outside, my visual field was moving all over the place. It felt like my vision was bouncing up and down with each step I took, making it extremely difficult to concentrate.

Another challenge I faced was pushing my body to its physical limit again. When my heart rate reached a certain level, my symptoms would start coming back. I would be fine all the way up until my heart rate got around 170 beats per minute (190 is my max), then I would become lightheaded, which led to dizziness. This frustrated me at first, but I learned it was normal. When you suffer a concussion, your brain basically gets reset. When you first try to come back and physically exert yourself, your brain isn't used to it, thinks it's bad, and tells your body to stop. In order to sustain a high level of physical exertion, you have to retrain your brain to realize that physical activity is OK, and that your body will be able to handle it.

This process took me a while, probably a month.

Because I had learned that these symptoms were common with athletes recovering from a concussion, I kept pushing on and retraining my brain. Eventually, my visual field became more stable and my body got used to working out again. Once this happened, I was finally ready to get back on the field and start playing soccer. I couldn't wait. I figured once I was able to run without any symptoms, everything else would be easy—specifically the soccer aspect. Unfortunately, I couldn't have been more wrong.

When I first returned to the field, I felt like I hadn't played soccer in five years. Everything I did felt different. Something as simple as controlling and passing the ball felt harder. Normally, I wouldn't have to think twice about controlling the ball and then passing it. It was muscle memory. After the concussion though, I felt like I had to focus extra hard (I actually had to look down at my feet) in order to successfully control and pass the ball.

I also struggled with my peripheral vision. When I returned

to playing, it felt like everything around me was happening so fast. Often, when an athlete goes through a successful period, he or she describes the game as "slowing down" for them. That was something I had experienced in the past. After the concussion, it was just the opposite. Everything seemed to speed up.

By late April, I returned to the starting lineup against San Jose. Going in, I felt good. I felt ready. Early in the match, I headed a cross away for a clearance. Right after that, I started experiencing some symptoms. I struggled with my vision, especially the stadium lights. I could feel and hear a constant buzz for the rest of the half. It was almost like my ears were echoing. As a result, I struggled to play at the level I was used to. I misread a through ball and then mistimed a tackle that caused me to receive a yellow card. Then I misread a ball that was lobbed up in the air, which caused a counter-attack. To top it all off, I lost two balls off the dribble when I mishandled a pass. Needless to say, I couldn't wait to hear the halftime whistle. During halftime, I got some water and allowed my body and heart rate to calm down. This helped a lot. After ten minutes in the locker room, the buzz and ringing went away. When I took the field for the second half, my vision had cleared and I was good to go for the rest of the game. However, I did end up getting subbed off with around fifteen minutes to play.

I'd hoped that my first game back would mark my return to form, but it clearly didn't. This was incredibly frustrating . . . and a little bit scary. It almost felt like I had to start over, like it was my first year as a professional. Soccer is a fast, free-flowing game that forces you to process information and make decisions on the fly. When you're not able to do that well, it becomes extremely difficult. I could barely tell if the person in my peripheral vision was on my team or not. How was I supposed to see movements, openings, and angles?

One of my strengths as a player is reading the game. A lot of times, I'm able to read another player and know where he's about to play the ball before he plays it. I can see his eyes, or see the angle of his hips, or the spin on the ball. This allows me to step up and intercept the ball, or make a recovery run into the space before the ball arrives. My game is basically built on reading the intention of the opponent. After the concussion, I wasn't able to do this like I had been used to. I felt like I was having trouble seeing and processing the tiny details that previously gave me an advantage.

Ultimately, I felt a step slow. I felt like I was reacting to things happening around me. I felt like I was misreading plays, which led to wrong decisions, which led to mistakes. All because I wasn't as mentally sharp as before. It's impossible to express how much this frustrated me. Was I ever going to read the game like I used to? What was going to happen if I couldn't see things I was normally used to seeing?

Fortunately, my instincts started coming back. Slowly. Gradually. It started out in practice. I would have good practices—days when I felt sharp, clear, and in control. I would also have bad practices—days when I felt slow, cloudy, and not myself. I didn't consistently feel good in game situations until after the summer, around September. The injury happened in March, so that's about five months of dealing with lingering symptoms.

As I mentioned before, when you suffer a concussion, your brain basically gets reset. To make it back to preconcussion levels, you have to retrain your brain. This takes repetition, which takes time. Understanding and accepting this gave me a bit of patience, but the recovery process was still frustrating and hard.

Toward the end of the year, I definitely knew I was back. The second I stepped on the field for warm-ups, I could feel it. I felt clear, confident, and calm. I knew I could make the plays I made before the concussion, and that made me feel excited. And relieved.

INSIGHT

If you haven't experienced a severe concussion, it's difficult to understand how difficult and lengthy the recovery can be. You might even think I'm exaggerating. I understand that, because not too long ago I was in your shoes. Still, I hope I've provided enough insight to help you understand the situation. And to those who have experienced or are currently dealing with the aftermath of concussion, I wish you the best and hope sharing my story will help in your own recovery.

Here are my three biggest takeaways from my concussion experience:

1. You will recover. You will feel better. I don't know when exactly that will be, or how long it will take. Each situation is different. I don't know what rehab techniques will work best for you. I don't know what hurdles will be most difficult for you. The only thing I can tell you for certain is you will eventually recover. You will eventually feel better. Trust that.

2. Take your time. This is something I didn't do. Looking back, it's a mistake I made. I felt pressure to take risks and come back as quickly as possible. I felt like my career was at stake, because when I'm not playing, my job is in jeopardy. Now, you may not feel as rushed to get back on a soccer field as I did, but I guarantee you'll feel pressure from somewhere— your job, your spouse, your friends, your financial demands—to accelerate the

recovery process. Don't fall into that trap. Take a step back and be patient. Don't worry if your road to recovery is different than someone else's, different from what a book or the Internet says, or even what the doctor says. It's going to be different.

3. Be honest with yourself. This will be hard. I think sometimes it's harder than being honest with others. But this is the only way you'll truly be able to recover. If you're feeling something, say it. If you have a setback, say it. Don't be scared. It's impossible for others to know exactly what's going on. Heck, it's even impossible for brain imaging scans to see everything that's going on. That's why your openness and honesty is so important. You are the single best resource for feedback and information.

As I write this, I can finally say I'm fully recovered. Some things took a few weeks to regain, some several months or longer. But I'm back to where I was before the injury. I can physically perform the way I want to. I can keep up with the speed of play and make decisions on the fly. I can see the game happening like I used to, and read plays beforehand. Most important, I'm back to being myself as a person. I no longer feel the uncertainty and anxiety of not knowing if I'll ever get better. I have confidence. I'm not afraid anymore.

To end this piece, I want to recognize the importance of my doctors and trainers. Along with many other people such as my family and friends, my doctors and trainers were by my side every step of the way. They followed the concussion protocol to a T and were thorough in everything they did. Whenever I had a question or concern, they went above and beyond in answering it. They exhausted options for rehab techniques, looking into anything that could possibly help me. No expense was spared. Throughout my recovery, no matter what, they always emphasized that my health was the most important thing. They made sure I never lost sight of that. Thank you. I'm forever in your debt.

The World Cup (and After)

THE GROUP OF DEATH, A GUT-WRENCHING LOSS, AND A GREAT BIG DECISION

"When you play in the World Cup, it stays with you for the rest of your life."

—MB5

MY FIRST WORLD CUP CAP: U.S. VS. GHANA, ESTADIO DAS DUNAS, JUNE 16, 2014

Walking onto the field for warm ups, I immediately felt a buzz in the stadium in Natal, Brazil. Everyone has heard that expression before, but it really is true—it's a feeling that's rare. Only a few other times in my career compare to what the stadium felt like that night: the MLS Cup 2013 in Kansas City, the World Cup qualifier against Mexico in Azteca in 2013, and the 2015 CONCACAF Cup Final in the Rose Bowl. The atmosphere was electric. As I walked onto the field, I felt alive.

During warm-ups, I ran back and forth across the field about twenty times to get loose. It wasn't planned, but my Kansas City teammate Graham Zusi ended up running right next to me the entire time. After we'd fallen into step together, I looked over at him. Maybe it was nervous energy, but I just started laughing. "How did we end up here?" I asked him. We had been through a lot together as professionals. Now, we were both about to play a World Cup match for our country. "We've come a long way from your parents' basement." Graham joked, referring to our rookie year when we lived together in my parents' basement to save money.

This brief exchange lasted only a few seconds, but that moment meant a lot and is one I will always remember. It helped me calm down. It gave me perspective and allowed me to go out and embrace the opportunity ahead. I was about to play in the biggest game of my life, but I wasn't that nervous. Having one of my best friends by my side to share the experience with was a major factor in helping me to relax.

I honestly don't remember much at all after the start of the game. The nerves and adrenaline probably caused my memory to go south. I do remember Clint Dempsey's goal thirty seconds into the game. I have no idea how it happened—all I remember is seeing him shoot across the goal and the ball hitting off the far post and into the net. The crowd erupted, and I sprinted sixty yards downfield to celebrate with him and the rest of my teammates. The next forty minutes were fairly uneventful, in large part because I don't really remember anything that happened. (Again, adrenaline makes it hard to remember sometimes.)

With a few minutes left to play before halftime, one of the midfielders from Ghana played a ball over the top of our defense and I was forced to chase it down. It was a thirty-yard sprint. I ran step for step with the Ghanaian forward. As we both arrived at the ball, I made a last-second lunge to slide and kick the ball out of bounds. Just as I made contact with the ball, I felt a sharp pain in my upper hamstring. Immediately, I reached around with my hand and felt a knot of tensed muscle about the size of a gumball where my hamstring and glute attach. I got the fight or flight response feeling of heightened adrenaline, and I felt the warmth of blood quickly rushing through my body. Fortunately, I made it the next few minutes to halftime without aggravating it any further.

When the halftime whistle sounded, I rushed straight into our locker room. I lay on the training table and our head trainer started taking a look, asking me questions. I did my best to explain what happened. I told him I thought my foot got caught underneath my body when I fully extended on the slide tackle, which probably caused my hamstring to strain. The plan was for him to massage and loosen the muscle up before the second half. We had fifteen minutes to get it back. As soon as he started working on it, the muscle began spasming. It got worse with any pressure he applied. He said, "Bes, I don't think we are going to be able to get this thing to calm down. It's spasming too much."

My stomach dropped. "I don't want to come out of the match," I said. "I'm going to try and play through it." That was my initial mind-set. I honestly felt like I could still make most of the plays I needed to make. The problem, I knew, was I'd be limited when

I opened up my stride and fully extended the hamstring. Time was running out before the start of the second half. We had to make a decision. I remember our trainer looking me straight in the eye telling me, "I know this sucks to hear, but in my professional opinion, I don't think you can go back out there for the second half. Your hamstring is too tight. You're one play away from completely tearing it." When I heard those words, I knew I had to take myself out of the game.

Immediately after informing our coach I couldn't play, I started to tear up. I had put in a tremendous amount of work and preparation for this moment, and I was scared I just suffered an injury in the first match of the World Cup. Terrible timing. Also, I felt like I had let down my family and everyone else back home watching. Even more so, I felt like I was letting my teammates down. I felt helpless, like everything was out of my hands. My World Cup dream was slipping away.

I sat by myself for a few minutes and gradually calmed down. Our trainer came back over to me and put his hand on my

"MY WIFE OFTEN REMINDS ME, 'THERE'S ALWAYS SOMEONE BETTER OFF THAN YOU. THERE'S ALWAYS SOMEONE WORSE OFF THAN YOU.'"

shoulder and said, "You made the right decision. I know you wanted to play, but you would be putting yourself at major risk for suffering a serious injury and jeopardizing your entire World Cup." He was right. By taking myself out, I gave myself a chance to come back and play later in the tournament. Our hope was the injury wouldn't be too serious, and I would be able to recover from it. This sliver of hope was all I needed to get me through that tough situation. I began looking forward.

I sat on the training table. I looked over and saw Jozy Altidore lying there, face down on the table across from me. Earlier in the half he also suffered a hamstring injury and was forced to leave the game. However, Jozy's injury was much more serious than mine. He was weeping, overcome with emotion.

He knew that, more than likely, his World Cup was finished. Here I was, feeling sorry for myself. Asking myself, why was this happening to *me*? How could God do this to *me*? Why now? It had all been about me while one of my teammates, who suffered a far more serious injury than I had, was lying there, too. I was feeling helpless, but I couldn't imagine what Jozy was going through. In that moment, I felt embarrassed. I felt ashamed and small for being so selfish. I remember shaking my head and telling myself to be stronger. I walked over to Jozy, put my arm around his shoulders, and told him, "I'm so sorry, brother."

After another five to ten minutes passed, Jozy and I walked out of the locker room together and made our way to the bench so we could watch the rest of the second half and support our teammates. With the match tied 1–1 for most of the second half, we scored a dramatic goal in the eighty-sixth minute. It was from a corner kick taken by Graham Zusi. The goal scorer? John Brooks, who replaced me at halftime. Seriously, you can't make this stuff up. In the moment he scored, all the pain, anxiety, and sadness with my injury went away. I was free to enjoy the moment and celebrate with the rest of my teammates.

Taking yourself out of a game is never easy. Some people might think you're selling out, you're not being tough, and it's "the easy thing to do." I believe just the opposite. Taking myself out of the game in such a big moment was scary. In my opinion, the easy thing would have been to not say anything so I wouldn't risk the possibility of having to come out and end my World Cup. Looking back, I know I made the right decision. I made the responsible decision for the good of the team. Me being on the field slightly injured, at 80 percent, would have been selfish. I would have put the team's success in jeopardy. To this day, it was one of the hardest

decisions I've ever had to make. I still feel intense emotions every single time I replay that situation in my head.

The next day, I went to a doctor in São Paulo to get an MRI scan on my hamstring. Fortunately, there was no tear in the muscle. This was the best-case scenario we were hoping for! Our next game was in six days, so I had a good chance to recover. My goal was to get myself back and be ready to contribute again. I spent hour after hour in the training room getting rounds of treatment. We knew my hamstring probably wasn't going to heal all the way in such a short time frame, so it wouldn't do any good to treat the actual hamstring (it might have made it worse by re-irritating it). Instead we focused on strengthening all the surrounding muscles, so when I played it would take the load off the hamstring. This strategy worked. When I went out to test the hamstring, two days before our next match, I passed the fitness test. It wasn't perfect, but the prep work we did with all the surrounding muscles helped shield the injury so my hamstring didn't have to work as much. The situation wasn't ideal and I didn't feel my best, but I felt comfortable enough to play. I was back, and available for our next match!

I owe so much thanks to our training staff who helped get me back. They went above and beyond their responsibilities. They gave me hope and kept me positive. And obviously, they did an unbelievable job with rehab, allowing me to get back on the field.

their second group stage match that day, and kickoff was scheduled in exactly two hours. The streets were packed. I've never seen anything like it. Cars couldn't move. People jammed the streets and the familiar yellow Brazilian soccer shirt was everywhere. I felt like our taxi was stuck in the middle of Carnival. People were partying, singing, dancing, and getting

"You have to show up in the World Cup, and in the World Cup anything can happen."
—Lionel Messi

One other memorable part of this experience was the drive to and from the MRI building. I took a taxi along with Jozy Altidore, our team doctor, and one of our security agents. The building was close, less than a mile away, but we needed to take a taxi since Jozy was on crutches. Plus, it wasn't a smart idea for two U.S. soccer players to walk down the middle of the street in São Paulo. The trip took two hours. I'm not exaggerating. We drove less than a mile in two hours! The reason? Brazil, the host country, played

ready to watch Brazil. Vendors hawking souvenirs and food were everywhere.

Once we finally arrived at the MRI office, we spent about an hour getting scanned and waiting to hear from the doctors. When we had the scans in hand, we hopped in the same taxi that had brought us and headed back to the hotel. The return trip took four minutes. Not kidding. I timed it. We even took the same route back. The same trip that took two hours just a short while ago, took only four minutes. The city was a complete ghost town—like one of those end-of-the-world apocalypse movies such as *I Am Legend* with Will Smith. No one was on the streets. No cars, no people, no vendors. I honestly had to stop for a second and ask myself if I was dreaming, or if this could really be the same city as a few hours earlier.

The reason, of course, was that the Brazil game was on. Everyone in the city was inside watching it. Even our taxi driver was watching. The driver had an iPad that he held up over his steering wheel so he could watch while he drove. I have no idea how he could see the road. It was seriously dangerous to be in that taxi. Luckily, there was no one in the street he could crash into.

In many ways, my injury enriched my overall World Cup experience, even that crazy day with the MRI. It gave me a once-in-a-lifetime, close-up look at the beating heart of a *fútbol* mad city in the middle of the soccer universe—a perspective I would never have had if I had not been injured. It's funny how things work out.

RIO MEMORIES

I get asked this question a lot: "What was your favorite part about the World Cup in Brazil?" This is a hard question to answer, because the experience was so incredibly rich and packed with excitement.

Obviously, being on the field and playing is one of my favorite memories. Singing the national anthem right before representing the country would also be right at the top of the list. But some of my favorite memories are of more private moments, and two stand out.

I recently watched the Olympic Games in Rio, and was reminded of how special it is to represent your country at a world sporting event. I watched athletes stand on the podium, tears rolling down their cheeks, as the U.S. national anthem played. This was their moment.

My moment didn't come on the field or on a podium in Brazil at the World Cup. My moment came in the locker room after a game. We had just finished our final group stage match against Germany and learned that we had advanced out of the Group of Death and into the Round of 16. Our team was in the locker room celebrating together, taking selfies, and playing music (mostly hip-hop). All of a sudden, Bruce Springsteen's "Born in the USA" came on. We cranked it up full blast and started singing along. It was such a rush—a high of emotion, pride, and adrenaline. It's ironic actually because not everyone on our team was born in the United States, but that didn't matter. Everyone knew the words. At that moment, I felt united with my teammates and proud as hell to represent my country. And since I

wasn't actually on the field playing, I was able to take a step back and soak it all in. That was *my* moment.

My other favorite memory was experiencing the atmosphere when Brazil, the host country, played a game. It was unreal! Most people are familiar with Brazil's national passion for soccer, but until you experience it firsthand, it's hard to truly appreciate.

When there was a match, the entire country shut down. You could feel the emotion in the streets. I vividly remember watching the opening match of the World Cup, Brazil vs. Croatia, from my hotel room in São Paulo. My room was on the twentieth floor, and my window was open. As I watched a fairly uneventful portion of the game, I suddenly heard an

eruption outside—a synchronized roar that seemed to travel for miles and miles all at once. It actually startled me. I thought possibly there had been an explosion.

Immediately, I looked back to my television and watched Neymar Jr. score his second goal of the game to give Brazil a 2-1 lead. My television feed was delayed by about five seconds from what the local Brazilians were watching.

Right after the roar, fireworks went off like crazy throughout the city. I got chills. For the rest of the tournament, a small part of me looked forward to the days Brazil had a game. And I made sure to watch each game with my window open.

THE 105ᵀᴴ MINUTE: U.S. VS. BELGIUM . . . FROM GLORIOUS TO GUT-WRENCHING

After advancing out of the Group of Death, we were set to face Belgium in the Round of 16. This was one of the most hyped games of the World Cup. The winner would advance to the quarterfinals to face Argentina. As a country, we had only made it to the quarterfinals of a World Cup once (2002), so this was a huge chance to match that performance, with the potential to go even further. I knew our team was ready for the opportunity. Everyone on the roster believed we could get the job done and find a way to win. The days leading up to the match were tense, but the confidence of our team kept growing.

To share my U.S. vs. Belgium experience, I decided to write two letters to my future self. These contain what I would say to myself, with the benefit of hindsight. The first letter is for me to open up **BEFORE** the Belgium game. The second letter would be for me to open up **AFTER** the Belgium game.

A letter from my future self to be opened the morning of our 2014 World Cup game against Belgium.

Dear Matt,

Bon dia! This morning when you wake up, you'll immediately realize what's at stake. You'll be able to feel it, and everyone around you will, too. You're about to play a World Cup Round of 16 match against Belgium, a top-five team in the world. Don't be intimidated though. You've already played two other top-five teams (Germany and Portugal), and you and your teammates found a way to advance from the Group of Death, a feat not many thought you could accomplish. So go into the game with confidence.

When you get to the stadium, take in as much as you can. Walk around the field before the game. Your wife, your parents, your brother, and your best friends will be at the stadium early, too. You'll see them behind one of the goals about twenty rows up. Go over and say hi to them! And smile for that picture your mom takes . . . it will end up being one of your favorite pictures taken during the World Cup.

When you line up in the tunnel right before kickoff, don't look across at Belgium. Their roster will be littered with talent. Up and down their line will be world-class players you sometimes watch on the weekends. Specifically, don't look across at Vincent Kompany, their captain. That dude is a physical specimen. If you look, your last thought will be you're about to go up against LeBron James in soccer cleats. That doesn't matter though. The only thing that matters is you're focused on yourself, your teammates, and this one game. In this one game, you will know it's possible to knock them off.

The match will start exactly how you imagined it would: Fast paced, wide open, and end to end. Remember, a few days ago in a team meeting when you guys went over the game plan? You decided your best chance was to really go after Belgium. Don't get pinned back like in the Germany game. Push up high. Attack them. If you're going to go down, at least go down swinging.

After about fifteen minutes, you'll settle into the game. You'll be in the zone. You'll be excited to find out that you'll be "feeling it" this game. This doesn't mean it will be easy though. Actually, just the opposite. You're going to be put under a lot of pressure. Belgium will come wave after wave, but you'll be ready. For most of the first half, you and your teammates will have to put out fires and defend counterattacks, but Belgium won't be able to get much past you.

And if they do . . . you have Tim Howard behind you. Let me back up again to the start of your day. When you wake up and go eat breakfast, find Tim Howard and see what he's eating for breakfast. Then, eat EXACTLY what he does! You won't understand this until after the game, but Tim Howard will have the game of his life. Actually, you'll realize this in about the sixtieth minute. Save, after save, after save, after save—sixteen in all, a World Cup record. He will be an absolute beast, and it will be an honor to share the field with him that day.

You'll be inspired by Timmy. His performance will give you extra energy to perform at your highest level possible. You will do everything you can to not give up shots, throwing your body around in order to keep that clean sheet. Remember something very important: If you can't make the play yourself, do everything you can to close down the angle on the shot. This will give Tim the best chance to make so many great saves. You will use this specific piece of advice a lot in this game, trust me!

You're welcome to stop reading this letter now if you don't want to spoil the ending, but I highly suggest you continue on.

After ninety minutes, the game will remain scoreless. You and your teammates will put in a gutsy performance and hold Belgium without a goal through regulation. You'll even have a chance to score in the last minute to win, but it won't be in the cards. That means you'll go into extra time. In the huddle before extra time starts, you'll look around at your teammates and you'll be able to see the belief in their eyes. Every single person will believe. No one will have any doubts. It will be an amazing feeling. You will truly feel like you're going to find a way to win this game and advance to the quarterfinals.

At the start of extra time, Belgium will make a substitution up top. Romelu Lukaku will enter the game. Pay attention to this moment, and understand that he's coming on fresh. And you're not.

Halfway through extra time, there will be a ball that pops out near midfield. For the entirety of the game so far, you've made every right decision. You've made every play and stepped up each time to win these balls. But here's the thing— don't try and win it this time. Even if you think you can win it, don't try! Because if you do, you'll underestimate Lukaku's ability to get to the ball before you, and you'll be a half second late. That half second will allow him to touch the ball first, you'll slip to the ground, and he'll take off toward your goal. Unfortunately, you and your teammates won't be able to recover on his run, and Kevin De Bruyne will eventually score about thirty seconds later to give Belgium a 1–0 lead.

In this moment, you won't think much about what just happened. You'll get on with the next play, just like you always do. You'll continue to fight, scratch, and claw for everything. You and your teammates will be exhausted. You'll be closer to throwing up and passing out than you've ever been before. Don't worry about that though; take your mind someplace else. Take it back to the United States where millions of people are watching. Make one more play, one more sprint for all those people back home. The American fight and spirit will allow you to dig deeper than you ever thought possible.

When the referee finally blows his whistle, Belgium will win the game 2–1. But not until after you and your teammates will almost fight back for an incredible comeback. You'll even have a chance to equalize on the very last play of the game, but it won't happen. That's sports sometimes. When it's finally over, you'll drop to your knees in devastation. You'll almost be too physically and emotionally drained to cry, even though that's what your body is trying to do.

What happens next, you'll remember forever. You'll finally get up, wipe away your tears, and walk over to your teammates to be with them. Tim Howard will come up to you, and before you can tell him that you're sorry for allowing Belgium to score, he will give you a giant bear hug, look you in the eyes, and say, "Hell of a game from you today, Matty. You should be proud. For me, you were one of the players of the tournament."

Try to let this sink in, Matt. It will be one of the most profound and powerful moments you'll ever experience on the field . . . or in life. Don't be too down about the loss to miss it.

Sincerely,
Your Future Self

A letter from my future self to be opened the morning after our 2014 World Cup game against Belgium.

Dear Matt,

This morning will be tough. It will be one of the hardest moments of your career so far. You have just been knocked out of the World Cup, in extra time, against Belgium. You and your teammates should be proud though. Both teams had their chances to win, and people will end up saying it was one of the most entertaining games of the entire World Cup. You'll know you represented your country in the best way possible, by giving everything you possibly had. You should be able to hold your head up high. Still, knowing this won't make today or the days to come any easier.

The pain is going to be real. It's going to hurt for a while: Days, weeks, and months. If I can tell you one thing that will help you get through this situation, it's to stay off social media for a while. It's going to be a nasty place. I know, you'll want to log on to acknowledge and thank the fans who were by your side the entire way, and the ones who will recognize the effort you and your teammates put in. However, it will be a place that's overshadowed by negativity. There will be hundreds of people lashing out at you, blaming you for the mistake you made on the play with Lukaku.

This will be extremely hard to deal with. It will almost crush you. It will make you sick to your stomach. You won't be able to get it out of your head. Instead of thinking about all the positives from the World Cup, you'll be stuck on this one negative. But don't give in. Stay strong in this moment. Deep down, stay true to yourself—trust yourself. You, along with your teammates, know that you had one of the best games of your entire life, and that's all that matters. Don't let a relatively small amount of people bring you so far down.

I'm afraid to tell you this, but unfortunately you might never be able to get away from people talking trash on you about that one play. I'm writing this letter to you almost three years later, and there are still people trying to bring you down. It's OK though. I promise you, life will go on. You'll eventually move forward. In fact, this experience will make you stronger. It will make you wiser. It will make you appreciate all the positive people in your life.

So, pick yourself up right now and get going with your day. Life isn't going to wait around for you to get over this loss. Pack up your bags, go meet up with your family, and get ready to fly back home. Here's one spoiler for you: When you land back in the United States, you're going to be overwhelmed by the reception you and your teammates receive. Be thankful for them. Focus on these people, not the social media haters.

Sincerely,
Your Future Self

"Shoot for the moon. Even if you fall short, you'll land among the stars."

In the house I grew up in, we had a loft/playroom upstairs that was designed for my brothers and me. It had wallpaper with hundreds of different quotes. That one was my favorite. It has always stayed with me and now made more sense than ever.

THE BIG QUESTION:
KANSAS CITY VS. EUROPE

Should I stay or should I go?
"Hey, so whatever happened when you thought about leaving Kansas City to play overseas? Why did you stay in KC?"

For a period of two or three years, this was the question I got asked the most by strangers on the street. It's also the question that annoyed me the most, because in the moment, there was no complete way to answer it. Nobody truly understood the situation, yet everyone had an opinion.

LET ME SET THE SCENE:

For many players, the World Cup is viewed as the ultimate showcase. It's the biggest opportunity they'll ever get to make a name for themselves. The entire world is watching: fans, scouts, coaches, owners, managers, anyone and everyone. Most players have the mentality that if you have a good tournament, your life will be changed. One good game and your name could be linked with clubs such as Chelsea, Manchester United, and Barcelona. One good half and you can potentially become a millionaire. Heck, even one good play and scouts and chairmen from clubs all over the world will start calling about you. Trust me, this stuff happens. I've witnessed it . . . and in 2014, I experienced it firsthand.

Going into the 2014 World Cup, I personally didn't think like this. Maybe I was naive, but my mind-set wasn't to play well so I could move to a bigger club and make more money. Those weren't my goals entering the tournament. I was solely focused on helping our team advance out of our group and make it as far as possible. Whatever happened as a result, I would handle when the time came.

It's safe to say I didn't fully understand the impact of playing in the World Cup. After the first game, against Ghana, my agent, Eddie Rock, received numerous calls from around the world. I was surprised by this because I'd been forced to leave the game at halftime due to injury. My guess is that by my simply playing in a World Cup game, teams were suddenly interested. That's the kind of credibility a World Cup cap gives you.

Fortunately, the injury I suffered against Ghana wasn't severe enough to keep me out, and I was able to play our second group match against Portugal. My reward for recovering quickly? I got to face off against Cristiano Ronaldo, considered by many to be the best player in the world at the time. In that match, Portugal wound up equalizing at 2–2 in the ninety-fifth minute, but it would still be our best team performance of the tournament. We had gone toe to toe with the third-ranked team in the world and opened many people's eyes by outplaying them. Individually, it was also one of my better games. I was proud to have been a part of the defense that frustrated Ronaldo for most of the game.

The performance didn't go unnoticed. Before the game was even over, Eddie's phone started ringing.

The next morning, I woke up to a voice mail asking me to call him back ASAP. More than a dozen teams had called, and Eddie briefly filled me in on some of the interest. I can't deny that it was exciting. However, after giving the situation some thought and having a few conversations, we both decided that for the duration of the rest of the World Cup, I should focus solely on playing. I didn't want to hear about any more calls. Eddie would handle all those distractions behind the scenes while I concentrated on my job on the field. We would figure things out when the tournament ended.

Obviously, we didn't achieve as much as we wanted, but we definitely surprised some people and gained the respect of millions of people around the world. I remember seeing a global statistic showing who people were cheering for (other than their native country), and our U.S. team was at the top. Because of our performance, a lot of players on the team were getting attention from clubs around the world, and I was one of them.

NARROWING THE OPTIONS

The first interaction I had with my agent after we had been eliminated was overwhelming. Eddie went through the list of teams that had contacted him, which included clubs from England, Germany, Russia, Belgium, and Mexico among other countries. It quickly became clear this was going to be a lot of information to process, so

I cut him off halfway through our phone conversation and told him to send me an e-mail so I could better evaluate things. When I got off the phone with him, my mind was racing. Up until this point, I never realistically imagined myself playing professional soccer in any country other than the United States. Now, it seemed I was going to have that opportunity. Playing professional soccer overseas is a dream for most kids . . . now I needed to decide if it was *my* dream.

As soon as I got Eddie's e-mail, I began researching. I googled every team, stadium, city, and fan base. You name it; I tried to look it up. I wanted to gather as much information as possible about every situation. (I never knew how valuable Wikipedia could be.) Amanda and I would go back and forth sending each other links with relevant information.

After a few days of this, the options started to winnow down to a manageable number. We eliminated certain opportunities for different reasons. And sometimes it worked the other way—teams that showed interest initially reconsidered for their own reasons.

A PARTNER'S PERSPECTIVE

When we got back to the states, we talked out every pro and con about making the move overseas. My only requests throughout the whole process were that we would get to keep our house in Kansas (we had just moved into our first home and loved it), and that our dog, Gipper, would get to come wherever we went. Beyond that, I was pretty open. The Fulham option definitely captured my imagination. When I was in college, I had studied abroad in London and fallen in love with the city. I was ecstatic about the idea of moving there.

On the other hand, Matt and I both grew up in Kansas City, and our families both lived there. I went to the University of Kansas, not far from Kansas City, and Matt got drafted by his hometown club, Sporting Kansas City. We are both rooted in Kansas City, and we love everything about this place.

We had conversation after conversation, discussing everything from living expenses to taxes, the Fulham team culture, the pay, job security, housing options . . . even whether Gipper would be able to make the trip. Having such a love for both cities, I naturally fell into the role of devil's advocate. And to be honest, I was probably the one pushing more heavily for Matt to make the move.

But Matt struggled with this decision. I remember him saying, "I feel like if I open a door on one, I am closing a door on the other." He felt that if he left his hometown and the MLS, he could never come back and be "that guy," the captain, the hometown kid, the solid mainstay in what was becoming such a great club. On the flip side, he felt that if he didn't go overseas, the opportunity would never present itself again.

—Amanda Besler

When everything was settled, the two opportunities that were most appealing to me were from Fulham (England) and Frankfurt (Germany).

Over the next few weeks, I knew I was going to have to make the decision to either pursue one of these opportunities in Europe or stay with Sporting KC. I didn't realize it would end up being one of the hardest decisions I'd ever had to make.

COMING HOME

When I finally returned to Kansas City after the World Cup, I had been away for nearly eight weeks. I won't say I completely forgot what home felt like (because I never will), but there was a small part of me that did. Eight weeks is a long time to be away from home, especially when you're going through a life-changing event like the World Cup.

Turning on to our street, I immediately got that "home sweet home" feeling. Anyone who's been away at college will know exactly what I'm talking about. It's the feeling you get when you pull up to your house after being away for the semester and realize that you missed it far more than you'd thought you did.

Just before we reached our driveway, I noticed the flags. There must have been one hundred of them . . . American flags lining our driveway, hanging from the house, waving in our front yard. To this day I don't know who was responsible for putting them there, but it was really a powerful sight to see—and a great indication of the strength of our neighborhood community. I was overcome with emotion. Amanda and I were alone, but I felt just as proud to be an American in that moment as when I sang the national anthem at the World Cup with millions of people watching a few days before. The flags waving in the wind with the sun shining on the red, white, and blue was like a scene from a movie.

Within five minutes, neighbors started coming outside to welcome us home. They offered to help bring our luggage in and asked if we needed anything. They told me how proud they were to watch me on TV during the World Cup. Kids on my street gave me posters they'd made, and I remember hearing a loud, "U-S-A" chant throughout the neighborhood. In that moment, being back home in Kansas City, I started to realize I was in a special situation.

CONTEMPLATING A DECISION

People always say to follow your gut in situations like these. My problem was that my gut kept switching! There were times I was truly leaning toward Europe, imagining what life might be like overseas. Then I would switch back and imagine staying in Kansas City to help my hometown win more championships.

The hardest part was that I felt like no matter what I decided, I was closing the door on one opportunity, for good. If I chose Europe, I would never be able to go back and play the prime of my career in my hometown. Sure, I could always come back home, even to play again, but it wouldn't be the same. Conversely, if I chose to stay, more than likely I would never be able to go to Europe and play. By the time I finished playing the prime of my career in KC, I would be considered too old to go overseas, especially as an American. I knew this was a once-in-a-lifetime opportunity. That's what made it so difficult.

I reached out to a few of my closest friends and family for advice, thinking it would help. But it actually made things worse. Everyone had a different opinion. I quickly realized it was best not to involve other people on this one. I had to make the decision for myself and my immediate family.

I remember my mom kept texting Amanda and asking for updates. We had to keep telling her to wait patiently. I think back on this now and laugh a little bit. "Hey, Mom, don't stress. We'll just casually let you know if we are going to be packing up our bags and heading to Europe for a few years." In hindsight, I can see why she kept texting.

"Wouldn't it be a dream to play in Europe?" my mom would ask? Yes! Of course it would. *But* I had another dream, too . . . to play the prime of my career in my hometown, to be the captain, and to win more championships for Kansas City. I admit that having competing dreams was a good problem to have—but it was still a problem. I had to decide which dream to follow and which one to leave behind.

A PIVOTAL MEETING

A few days after I returned from Brazil, Sporting KC had a home game against the Chicago Fire. Peter Vermes and I decided that it was in the best interest for all parties for me not to play. The main reason was to get a few more days' rest from the grueling two months I had just experienced. Also, it was probably smart to take a break mentally with everything else that was going on.

Leading up to this point, Robb Heineman, one of our owners, was very open and honest with me. He reassured me that he understood my situation, and the ambition of many soccer players to play in Europe. He made it clear that the club only wants players who want to be here, and that if playing somewhere else was a dream of mine, he would work with me to make it happen (as he had shown in the past with a few other players).

During the Chicago game, I sat up in the owner's box next to Cliff Illig, another owner. We made small talk for a bit, but then we got down to the matter at hand. The first thing he told me was, "I want to be clear. We want you in Kansas City." This was nice to hear

from an owner. However, he told me, at the end of the day, this is a business and they have to be smart about what they do. The owners had built a club on certain principles, and they were only willing to compromise so much. They had to stay true to the system that had gotten them to this point. I understood this, and respected him for honestly laying it out as he did.

We talked for a bit longer, and at the end, he left me with a question: "Other than the actual contract, is there anything else you want in order to stay in KC?" He told me to think about it, to let him know, and he would do whatever he could to make that happen.

This question threw me off guard a bit. Up until then, it was natural to focus most of my thoughts on the traditional aspects of the contract, like salary, bonuses, and duration. But those were all factors that could apply anywhere, to any team. After thinking about Cliff's question and considering what really mattered to me and Amanda, I knew what to ask for. If I was going to pledge the prime of my career to Kansas City, then I knew I wanted to get more involved with the community. Amanda and

I did some volunteer work already, but actually establishing a charity would help us get more organized and be more effective in the time we gave. With that in mind, I worked with my agent, Eddie, to come up with a proposal that included provisions for establishing a charity right in the contract. We sent it to Sporting and waited to hear back.

RESOLUTION

After a few more days, I made my final decision. I would be staying in Kansas City to sign a long-term contract with Sporting KC.

Even with a couple years' perspective, I still can't pinpoint exactly what swung my decision. After all the back and forth, suddenly one day I just had a feeling that staying was the right thing to do.

A PARTNER'S PERSPECTIVE, PART TWO

Deep down, I knew Matt was not sold on the idea of going overseas. Maybe it was because, after being away so long, we returned home from Brazil on July 4th, the most patriotic holiday of the year; or maybe it was because Matt knew his heart was here and he would regret leaving.

Ultimately, Matt made the decision for himself. Not for anyone else besides himself and our family. So many people, especially those who don't really know soccer or Matt, were astonished by his decision. They could not believe that any player would choose to stay in the MLS and not take the opportunity to play in the sacred and praised English Premier League. We each had to "explain" our reasoning to many people in the following months, but those people who know Matt best were least surprised by his decision. Matt is a happier and better player because of his decision, and we are a happier and better family.

—Amanda Besler

I guess it came down to this. I kept asking myself, "Are you currently happy?" The answer was yes. And not just happy—the happiest I had ever been. So why would I want to leave that?

Another thing that made my decision easier was the fact the ownership group was making a significant investment in me, both financially and in number of years. It meant a lot to me because I know they take decisions like this very seriously, and it showed they believe in me as a player and person. Trust me, this is a great feeling to have as a player. When you know the ownership group of the club you represent believes in you personally, it makes it very easy to come to work every day and give everything you have to succeed.

The final factor was the team's commitment to charity. As I mentioned before, Cliff Illig inspired me with the idea to include a vehicle for establishing my own charity, the Besler Family Foundation, in the contract.

This may not seem like a big deal, but for me and my family, it was the cherry on top of the sundae. Not only would Sporting KC help me with getting everything up and running, they would make an initial donation of $50,000. To my knowledge, this is the first time something like this has been done before in professional sports. Organizations help their athletes all the time with charities, but the fact that they were willing to include it in my contract and make an initial generous donation shows what kind of club Sporting KC is. And what kind of people the owners are.

Once I re-signed with Sporting KC, I didn't really think about Europe and what could have been. I made my decision, and I looked forward. All I wanted to do was get back to work and get back on the field. As much as I tried to enjoy the process and not take for granted my "time in the spotlight," I honestly didn't enjoy everything else that came with signing a Designated Player contract. All the media attention focused on me and my personal situation made me feel a bit uncomfortable. It was a relief to get back to work.

One day I'm sure I may look back and wonder what the other door might have held, but for right now, I'm happy to focus on winning more championships for Kansas City.

One thing to note about this entire situation is that I was not a free agent through this process. People might think this was a decision like picking a college or choosing between Chevy and Ford. That's incorrect. It's not like I could just go around the world and pick a team to play for. I was under contract and legally obligated to play for Sporting KC until my contract ran out (two more years).

The only way for me to have moved was if another team offered Sporting KC and Major League Soccer a transfer fee. This provided a whole different set of obstacles. If Sporting KC really wanted to, they could have done nothing. They didn't have to offer me a new contract. They could have said right from the beginning they weren't going to allow me to entertain the idea of talking to other teams from Europe.

But they didn't do this. They understood the situation, handled things with pure class, and were professional throughout the entire process. For me, that's further confirmation that I made the right choice.

I'm grateful for the belief Sporting KC has shown in me and I work every single day not to let them down.

BACKLASH

When I re-signed with Kansas City, I thought I would simply go back to playing without much attention or backlash. I was wrong.

Sure, lots of people were happy I stayed with my hometown club, and I was grateful for them. For example, I ran into one of my former next-door neighbors (about thirty years older than me), and he told me how impressed he was with my decision. "You're a great role model for any kid growing up in Kansas City, and I've admired how you've handled yourself and stayed so loyal throughout your career." This felt good to hear, especially coming from someone I knew well and respected.

However, there were also a lot of people who criticized my decision to stay. That's OK. I figured there would be criticism, but it struck me as funny that so many people who didn't know me or know my motivations thought they knew what was best for me.

SOME OF THE CRITICISM I HEARD:

"How could he turn down the money in Europe? Isn't it way better over there?"

"He's not going to get better staying here. He must not have any ambition."

"He's scared to go over to Europe and try something different."

"He's already accomplished all there is to accomplish here. Why wouldn't he want to take on a new challenge?"

I never responded to any of this second-guessing online or in the media. I understand that passionate sports fans will always have their opinions and there's not much point in arguing. (It's even one of the things that makes pro sports so much fun as a fan.) But this is probably a good place to address some of the criticisms I heard at the time.

Yes, you typically get paid more in Europe than you do in MLS. And, sure, that was a factor to consider. But money isn't everything. It definitely wasn't the most important thing for me. It's also important to understand that just because you get paid more up front, doesn't always mean you end up with more. You have to consider taxes, cost of living, bonuses, and benefits.

Yes, many of the world's best players are in Europe. The standards and competition level are extremely high, so I understand how someone can make the argument that you can only get better by playing in Europe. But I firmly believe you can develop in MLS just as well as in Europe. It's all about having the right mentality. MLS will challenge you in different ways than Europe, just as Europe will challenge you in different ways than MLS. So anyone who thinks the only way to get better is to go over to Europe is wrong.

The MLS is challenging. The travel is a major obstacle. MLS teams log more travel miles than teams in any other soccer league anywhere in the world. I also think the parity throughout the league is the best in the world. On any given night, any team can beat another. It doesn't matter where you are in the standings, where you're playing, or who's injured. You have to bring it every single game or you will lose. The MLS style of play is fast paced.

It's physical and aggressive, with a lot of turnovers and transitions. That demands a lot of your body. Some international players aren't used to this and have difficulty keeping up in MLS.

Some people said I chose to stay in KC because it was the easy thing to do. They believed I'd rather stay in my comfort zone than face the pressure of playing in Europe. That's just not true and, actually, I knew I would experience something completely opposite of that. I'm not denying the pressures of playing in Europe. Of course there's pressure. The culture, the spotlight, the money, the fans . . . it's all there. But people who think players who play in MLS don't have any pressure are wrong. It might be a different kind of pressure than Europe, but it's still pressure. And it's real.

I signed long term with Kansas City because I wanted to push myself out of my comfort zone. I knew I would be held to the highest standard every single day, and that would be a challenge. I would be expected to be one of the best players in training every single day. I would be expected to be one of the best players on the field every single game. If not, I would be called out,

and deservedly so. That's pressure— to have the highest expectation and be held accountable for that every single day.

I also wanted to challenge myself to become a better leader. If I went to Europe, more than likely I would not have the same leadership responsibilities as I do now. I wanted these responsibilities. I wanted the highest expectations. I wanted to challenge myself to become a better player, leader, and person. I feel these responsibilities every single day.

Finally, I believed—and still believe—that we as a team and I as a player have more to accomplish in Kansas City. Yes, we've already accomplished a lot. As a team we've won an MLS Cup Championship and an Open Cup Championship, and I've played in all-star games and been named to the Best XI. But I want more. I shake my head at people who questioned me staying because "I've already accomplished everything there is to accomplish in KC." That's a bunch of garbage. I don't think like that! There's *always* something more to accomplish. There's *always* a new challenge. Bottom line, I want more championships with Kansas City; I want to establish a dynasty.

In the July 21, 2014, issue of the *Kansas City Star*, I wrote an open letter to my hometown.

Dear Kansas City,

Thank you. I grew up in front of you. You drafted me out of college and brought me home. You never turned your back on me while I learned the ins and outs of the professional game. You've provided the most loyal fans in MLS. You've made Sporting Park the best stadium in the country. You supported me with the U.S. National Team like I am one of your sons. You've reassured me that I am right where I belong.

There were many factors in deciding to re-sign long term with Sporting, but it starts and ends with the people of Kansas City.

On game day when I look around our stadium, it's mostly a blur of Sporting blue. But sometimes, I make eye contact with a person for a split second, and realize it's a friend. Sometimes I see family members and neighbors. I recognize teammates I used to play with, and rivals I used to play against. I see old teachers, coaches, and classmates. I see fans that started out as strangers, but are now friends.

It gives me chills knowing I get to play in front of all these people. It's truly an honor. After the game when I walk around the field and see so many familiar faces, all I can do is smile. Believe me, I don't take for granted the opportunity to play for you and our city.

I grew up idolizing many Kansas City sports figures. They were my heroes. When I first learned how to play baseball, I threw right-handed, but I started batting left-handed because that's what George Brett did on TV. To this day, I do everything right-handed, except for swinging a bat.

Just as my idols were, I am blessed to play a professional sport, not to mention in my hometown. There are many times when I feel like I should pinch myself, but the most powerful moments are when a kid comes up to me and asks for an autograph. Usually, when I finish writing my signature, their face lights up and they say, "Thank you Mr. Besler." But sometimes they say, "One day, I want to grow up and be just like you. You're my hero." If only they realized I was standing in their shoes 20 years ago.

I must thank the entire staff and the ownership group of Sporting Kansas City. There are hundreds of people who contribute to our success. Without a doubt, we have the best owners in professional sports. Their commitment and loyalty throughout this process is unmatched. Everyone should be excited at their vision and what we will accomplish together over the next five years. I am forever grateful that this organization is giving me the opportunity to play the prime of my career in my hometown.

Now it's time to get back to work. I have remarkable teammates and we have a chance to do something special. More than ever, we are motivated to win championships.

Thank you, Kansas City.
#SKC4LIFE

When I made my decision, I took one of the most popular chants from the best fans in the league to heart. It goes, "No other club! But SKC! For the glory of the city!"

It always gives me chills to hear it at Children's Mercy Park—for me, it was no other club than SKC... and no other home than Kansas City.

"All the stuff I learned as a kid on the baseball field, in backyard football games, and on the basketball court . . . I take it all out on the soccer field with me each day. It's all there."

Kids and Sports

LETTING KIDS LEAD, KEEPING PARENTS SANE, AND PUTTING FUN FIRST

"Their job is to play. Ours is to cheer them and love them. That's it."

— MB 5

ADVICE FOR KIDS AND PARENTS

Honestly, I could write an entire book about this subject, but I'll do my best to give you my thoughts and advice in a nutshell.

KIDS SHOULD PLAY MULTIPLE SPORTS.

(I know. All caps and bold type—that's pretty strong stuff. But I feel really passionate about this.)

In today's world, it's saddening to see how much pressure we put on kids to "specialize" in one particular sport at such a young age. What's the point of this? Will it really make them better? I believe that making kids specialize in one sport or activity does more harm than good. It's a message both kids and their parents need to understand.

Dear Parents,

BALANCE OR BURN OUT? The obvious danger of specializing is burning a kid out. Think back to when you were a kid. If you did something for too long, over and over again, you would eventually get sick of it, right? And, if you were forced by someone else to do something for too long, over and over again, it would make you want to stop even more, right? This applies to sports. Please don't make kids specialize too early. They will get burned out. They will stop playing. And you'll regret it.

You might say, "Well, I'm not pushing my kid to make any decisions to specialize. They're doing it all on their own. They're choosing to practice ten hours a week. They want to!" If this is the case, I suggest you take a step back and honestly assess the situation. Are you positive you're not influencing your kid? Because I know when I was a kid, I subconsciously felt pressure from my parents. I think all kids do. Even though my parents never forced me to do anything, I still felt pressure to make them happy and proud. It's only natural.

In my opinion, even if your kid says he or she wants to specialize in something at an early age, I would do my best to limit that activity and keep a good balance with other activities. Your child will become better rounded as an individual, and over time, will naturally discover their greatest passions and talents.

CREATE A BETTER-ROUNDED PERSON. Encouraging and allowing your kid to play multiple sports will do wonders for their development as a person. It will open them up to different techniques, demands, and disciplines. Also, it will expose them to different coaches. This is huge developmentally. A football coach is going to be completely different than a soccer coach. A basketball coach will likely have a different style than a golf coach. What an opportunity for your kid to learn the skills of adapting to different coaches and people! Every coach I've ever had has shaped me in some way. My approach to sports (and a big part of my outlook on life) has been molded by all my different coaches. I feel fortunate and grateful to have experienced such a broad range of influences.

HAPPINESS IS THE ULTIMATE GOAL. I get it. We all want to see our kids reach their maximum potential. But please don't feel like you have to push them in a certain direction in order to do so. Don't be scared that they'll someday resent you if they don't become a professional athlete.

"CHILDREN NEED THE FREEDOM AND TIME TO PLAY. PLAY IS NOT A LUXURY. PLAY IS A NECESSITY."

—Kay Redfield Jamison, professor of psychiatry

Which scenario do you think is more likely? Your kid comes to you in twenty years and says, "I'm disappointed in you, Mom and Dad, for not forcing me to specialize in basketball when I was younger. I could have been Michael Jordan if it wasn't for you!" Or, they come to you, with a healthy perspective, and say, "Thank you, Mom and Dad, for letting me play what I wanted to play and figure out what I like to do on my own. It was a blast."

Sure, that exact conversation might never happen, but you get the point. If you're still not convinced, here's a little more insight gained from my experiences playing soccer collegiately, professionally, and internationally. I would guess that 90 percent of my teammates who made it to these levels did NOT specialize in soccer at an early age. It's very rare to see someone who didn't play other sports growing up. Even further, I've noticed that guys who grew up playing multiple sports are actually better overall athletes and more balanced as individuals.

One more point: Don't become obsessed with finding that college scholarship. I promise, if your kid is good enough, the scholarship will somehow find a way to your kid. Forcing them to specialize isn't going to speed up the process or help in any way.

—Matt Besler

Dear Kids,

PLAY! TRY NEW SPORTS! Even if you've never played a certain sport before or think you won't be good at it, give it a try! You'll never know what it's like unless you experience it. Worst case, you play it for a season and decide not to play again the following year.

DON'T BE AFRAID TO TRY SOMETHING NEW. Take a chance to get out of your comfort zone. Twenty years from now, you'll think back to that time you convinced your parents to let you play ice hockey for one season and laugh. You weren't very good, and you clearly didn't make it to the NHL, but you know what? You learned a lot from that experience. You learned how to skate, you learned how to explain what icing is, and you even have a scar that you can show off during the holidays from the time you took a puck to the chin. These are the memories and experiences that will stick with you forever!

BECOME A BETTER ATHLETE, PHYSICALLY. Not only will you create memories to last a lifetime, you'll actually become a better all-around athlete by playing multiple sports. Challenge yourself to become good at as many sports as possible. Each sport challenges your body in specific ways. For example, if you're really passionate about basketball, you should play it in the winter, but in the spring you should run cross-country. That may sound crazy. After all, on

Don't compare yourself to anyone else. Trust me, it doesn't matter how many lessons your neighbor is taking, or where your classmate in school gets to travel for tournaments. Just because someone else is practicing more or paying more doesn't mean they will make it further than you. And just because someone is on a better team than you doesn't mean they're automatically better. Everyone is different, and there's no blueprint on how to succeed in sports. Focus on developing into the best version of yourself, while enjoying the process. There's no point in putting in all this work if you can't have fun at the same time.

the basketball court you never have to run longer than a sprint. But that's exactly my point. By only practicing basketball, you're limiting yourself and your body as an athlete. Running long distance will expand your body's capacity to perform. It will help you in more ways than you can imagine.

BECOME A BETTER ATHLETE, MENTALLY. Playing multiple sports will also make you mentally stronger. The mental side of the game is just as important as the physical side. Just as long-distance running presents a different set of physical challenges from basketball, it also requires—and develops—different mental conditioning. Any athlete who has experienced the solitary nature of a long run—whether in competition or not—knows that it takes your head to a totally different place. Other sports—baseball, bowling, cycling—all require different mental approaches. They're all great sports, but they're even better when they're not your only physical outlet. Variety in physical activity is a lot like variety in your diet. Balance—and, yes, moderation, too— will serve you best in the long run. It's also a lot more fun.

—**Matt Besler**

MY LIFE AS A SPORTY KID

I know with 100 percent certainty that I would not be where I am today if it wasn't for playing multiple sports as a kid. I've learned countless lessons and developed many skills from the different sports I played. Combining all those experiences makes me who I am as an athlete and a person. I could go on and on with examples, but here's a short list of some of the ways playing multiple sports has helped me become a better professional soccer player.

BASEBALL

I played baseball every summer until high school. Baseball is much slower than soccer, but it requires a ton of discipline and preparation. Playing baseball taught me how to improve through repetition. I still miss those long practices on summer evenings fielding ground balls, catching pop flies, and taking batting practice, and doing it over and over and over again.

I also learned what it feels like to be a perfectionist, which is a good thing in sports. I had a rule for myself—before I could go home from practice, I had to successfully field ten grounders in a row, cleanly, without committing any mistakes. If there was just one small bobble, I had to start all over again. The memory of my dad with a bucket of balls standing at home plate, swinging away with his fungo bat, will never leave me. In soccer, I often do a technical drill with a partner who throws the ball, and I have to kick it back in the air. Twenty reps with each foot. Inside of the foot, outside of the foot, instep, thighs, chest, headers . . . there are plenty of variations. Just like when I was a kid, I still have the urge to start all over again if I mess up on one rep. I can thank baseball for introducing me to and instilling in me the notion of "striving for perfection."

Through baseball, I also learned how to think ahead during competition. Many other sports rely on athleticism and instincts, but in baseball, you have to be tuned into the game to a greater degree than any other sport. At all times, you have to know the situation. What's the score? What inning? What's the count? How many outs? Who's on base? If the ball is hit to me in the air, where do I throw it? What if it's hit to me on the ground? Where do I need to be for the cutoff? What happens if someone tries to steal? I had to ask and answer these questions in my head before each pitch. Baseball requires you to be locked in mentally, for every second of the game. If you're not, you'll make a mistake.

This skill has directly translated to the soccer field. Sporting KC's head coach, Peter Vermes, describes it as "being locked in for every roll of the ball." In soccer, the situation is constantly changing with every play. You have to be aware and ready at all times. When the ball goes out of bounds, it's not a

time to rest. When the ref blows the whistle for a foul, it's not a time to relax. These are the moments you have to be assessing and thinking about the game and what you're supposed to be doing—going through your mental checklist, just like in baseball. I'm so thankful I had the opportunity to learn this habit through baseball at a young age.

FOOTBALL

I only played football for one year, in seventh grade, but I played all the time in the backyard with my brothers and friends. The game we played the most was called "Offense Defense." Three people play: one quarterback, one receiver, and one defensive back. Simply, it was one on one. You try and beat your man, over and over again. I believe playing this game helped develop a part of my mentality as an athlete. This is where I was first introduced to playing mind games with somebody and trying to win the psychological battle over him.

Of course, this game also had great benefits from an athletic standpoint. An important part of most sports is "getting open." How do you practice getting open? Football is a great start. You learn how to shift, fake, juke, and change speeds to create space for yourself.

Additionally, football taught me how to judge distance to a ball in the air. This comes in handy in soccer, especially as a defender. When a long ball is played over the top, you must judge where the ball is going to land in order to run to the right spot and arrive before the ball (and the opposing forward). You have to run while looking up to track the ball, which is the same thing you do in football when someone throws you a long pass. When someone misses a header in soccer, it's usually because he or she misjudged the flight of the ball.

BASKETBALL

I played basketball every winter (and a few AAU summers) until my junior year of high school. Of all the sports I played, I believe basketball translates the best to helping you become a better soccer player, and vice versa. It all starts with footwork. Basketball requires a lot of quick movements, changes of direction, and stops and starts. People who play basketball at a young age will improve their coordination, quickness, agility, and balance. All are major assets

to have on the soccer field. I always get a kick (no pun intended) out of hearing the story of the seven-foot NBA player that has incredible footwork and can run up and down the floor like a gazelle. They always mention at the end how he got his start in soccer . . . of course he did!

One particular skill I learned through basketball was how to defend while using your peripheral vision. In basketball, when you're guarding someone on defense, you're always taught to know where the man is, as well as the ball. "One eye on the ball, one eye on your man, at all times!" our coach always used to say. This translates almost perfectly to soccer. In soccer, you always have to know where the ball is, but you also have to know where the opponents are around you. It takes skill to be able to move around and turn your body while also using your peripheral vision to see what's going on with the ball. It's funny, almost once a year there's a trialist that comes in from some foreign country, and it's very evident they've never played basketball before. Why? Because when it's time to defend, they think they have to go right up to their man and stay with them the whole time. They have their body turned the wrong way so they can't see the ball, and they're just running around face guarding the whole time. That's wrong. Remember, you have to see your man *and* the ball at all times.

Basketball also introduced me to the concept of zone defense. Depending on how your soccer team plays, this can be very helpful.

Finally, there's a habit I picked up from basketball that I still use today in soccer. When I was younger, I quickly learned that if I guarded my opponent too closely, he would never end up getting the ball, and I would never have the chance to steal it from him. Although that might be considered good defense, it was too boring for me. I wanted more action. When someone else from the opposing team had the ball, I learned to sag off my man just a bit, to make it appear like he was open. Then I would act like I wasn't really paying attention while watching the ball out of the corner of my eye. Right before the opponent tried to pass it to the player I was guarding, I would come alive, step into the passing lane, and steal the ball. I made a living off this! Lots of steals and breakaway layups. It was all about anticipation.

Although I don't use this strategy as often as I did on the basketball court, I still find myself doing it every so often when I play soccer. I like to bait the opponent into playing a pass they think is open, but in my mind I know it's coming, so I can step right into the passing lane and pick it off. One of the skills a good defender has to develop is anticipation. Anticipation, or always being in the right spot, is what makes the game look easy. I humbly like to think this is one of the strongest areas of my game, and I learned it playing basketball.

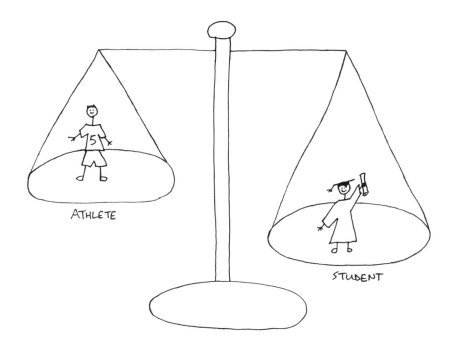

ATHLETE

STUDENT

KEEPING THE "STUDENT" IN "STUDENT-ATHLETE"

Recently, I went back to my alma mater, the University of Notre Dame, to be honored at halftime of a football game for being the first player from the school's men's soccer program to play in the World Cup. The university awarded me a plaque listing my college accomplishments. After the ceremony, I took time to go down the list, thinking about what each accolade meant to me. As I was doing this, my parents looked over my shoulder at the list and asked, "Which one of these are you most proud of?"

I started thinking to myself. All-American? Yeah, that might be at the top. First Irish player to play in the World Cup? Yeah, that would definitely give me some bragging

> **Why not add "being a good student" to your overall commitment of becoming a good athlete? Add it to the mix of other essentials like practicing, stretching, lifting weights, studying film, and eating healthily. When you put academics on the same level as all these other habits, you'll start caring more.**

rights around campus. All-Big East? Team MVP? Captain? Hmm . . . I could make a case for each one.

None of these was the winner, though. What I'm most proud of from my time at Notre Dame is what I accomplished academically. My senior year, I was named the NSCAA Scholar Athlete of the Year. That same season, I became the first person in Notre Dame athletic history to be named first-team All-American and first-team Academic All-American in the same year.

The reason I mention it is because I feel it shines a light on something very important—especially for young athletes.

To all the student-athletes out there, while you're busy making goals for your future, make sure you don't neglect the "student" part of "student-athlete." If you can strike the right balance and truly excel on the field (or court or pool, etc.) *and* in the classroom, it will mean more to you than any purely athletic achievement.

I know a lot of students will think that sounds impossible—that you can be either a good student or a good athlete, but not both at the same time. I'm here to tell you, that's not the case. Please don't fall into the trap of thinking you have to choose one or the other. If you really want to stand out, if you really want to separate yourself from others, make it a goal to do both!

The benefits to doing so will last long after your athletic career is over. Let me explain what I mean.

To this day, I feel I'm still reaping the benefits of dedicating myself to becoming the best student I could possibly be. Being a good student earlier in my life has given me the confidence to make smart "adult" decisions. Things such as buying a car, creating a financial budget, and learning about mortgages are all fairly intimidating at first. However, I know I'm capable of learning about each one and applying that knowledge to make good decisions. How do I know I'm capable? Because I've done it before! Throughout my academic career, I proved to myself that I can do it if I care enough and put forth the effort.

Being a good student will also open up far more job opportunities. Simply stated, the better you are time management, self-discipline, and a strong work ethic will serve you every single day of your life. I didn't realize at the time how choosing to be a good student would develop these habits, but now I do, and I'm so thankful I made the choice to place a high value on academics.

I don't expect you to realize all these benefits right away. I don't expect you to say in middle school that you want to get good grades

> **"Preparation is everything. The game is usually won before it's played. Are you prepared? Apply this lesson to any aspect of life and see what happens."**

academically, the more likely you are to find a good job. Trust me—when someone reads your résumé and sees you played sports *and* still performed academically, they'll think, "Wow, this person really has it together." Remember, not many people choose to do both, so this will be a major advantage for you.

Finally, and most importantly, being a good student has helped me develop good habits. Effective because it will help you with job opportunities after college. It's OK if your motivation for making good grades is something else—like your parents rewarding you with a trip to get ice cream (or even a little cash) for straight As. I don't realistically expect you to say in high school that you want to make good grades so you can be better prepared for buying a car, managing a budget, or understanding a mortgage.

It's more likely that in high school, you'll be motivated to make good grades simply because you want a high GPA to better position yourself for college. But the reasons why don't really matter.

All that matters is you make the decision to put academics high on your list. Because if you do, you'll benefit from it. And eventually, you'll start realizing the long-term benefits, just like I'm doing now.

TWO SIMPLE STEPS TO BECOMING A GOOD STUDENT-ATHLETE

1. DECIDE. Decide on the very first day of school that you want to be a good student-athlete. If you do, you'll already be ahead of half the students. Secret: Most of your peers will never decide if they want to be good at school or not. They will just go along with the flow. If they do well, great; If they do poorly, no worries. And if they do really poorly, they'll blame it on not really caring whether they're a good student or not. That's weak sauce. The funny thing is, they'll eventually look back and wish they would have made the decision to be a good student from the beginning. But you can't go back. So start now!

2. WORK. I firmly believe that being a good student-athlete is a choice. But, of course, there's more to it than just deciding. That's the first step. The second step won't surprise you. Work. Work like crazy to make it happen. It isn't easy, but I'm living proof that it's possible. Will you run into a teacher who seems to have it out for you along the way? Probably. Will there be a class or a concept that threatens to defeat you? Most likely. But if you've made the conscious decision to be a good student and you're willing to put in the work, you'll find a way to get through those moments.

Once you decide, your actions will choose themselves, which will set you up for success!

HOW TO GET THE MOST OUT OF A YOUTH SPORTS CAMP

For anyone who wants to play a sport at a level beyond recreational (club, academy, college, professional), you will probably find yourself attending some kind of camp or competitive out-of-town tournament. Of course, attending a camp or tournament doesn't guarantee you anything. On the other hand, it also doesn't mean you won't advance to the next level if you *don't* attend. But in my opinion, camps and tournaments will help you improve as a player and as a person. They will challenge you. They will help you get noticed by coaches who scout these events.

Here are a few tips on how to get the most out of a camp or tournament, and (with a little luck) how to get noticed by coaches:

1. Have an open mind.
Things won't go perfectly. There are going to be ups and downs. Accept this going in. Remember, you're gaining invaluable experience. You're learning what it's like to compete with other players in a more high-stakes setting with coaches and scouts around. The more experiences you can get like this, the more comfortable you'll be the next time you're in one of these competitive environments.

2. Learn.
There will be learning opportunities everywhere you look. Take advantage! Be like a sponge and soak up everything you can. If you really want to take it to the next level, bring a journal and each night write down five things you learned that day.

Don't just learn from coaches and instructors. Learn from everyone around you. Learn from your teammates. Observe what other players do in certain situations—how they warm up, their skills, their techniques. Sometimes you'll learn more from them than a coach. (Sorry, coaches!)

Don't just learn on the field or court. Learn how to carry yourself off the field—how to recover, how to stretch properly. Learn about good eating habits. This isn't just a chance to get better on the field; it's a chance to become a more complete athlete.

3. **Remember, you're making an impression on someone with EVERYTHING you do.**
    A. On the field or court
    B. How you warm up
    C. Your attitude toward teammates and opponents
    D. Your attitude toward coaches
    E. How you deal with a mistake or loss
    F. How you handle success or a win

This'll be our secret, but a lot of coaches actually look more for some of these intangibles (B–F) than performance (A).

4. **Relax. On field performance.**
This might be most important. The key is to find the right balance between trying to impress and just going out and playing. Don't think about scouts and coaches the whole time. You will perform your best if you're relaxed and confident. It's likely that finding this balance will require the experience of going through it a few times.

5. **Go to bed early.**
Don't worry what everyone else is doing. Nothing good happens after midnight anyway.

6. **Smile. Enjoy it!**
No matter the circumstances, keep this in mind. A smile can go a long way!

HIGH SCHOOL HEARTBREAK

What's your biggest regret in high school? Not studying enough? Not asking your crush to homecoming? Lying to your parents?

Mine was deciding to quit basketball. Seriously, out of all the regrets I have and mistakes I made in high school, that one is the biggest. I think about it all the time and wish I could have that decision back.

I loved basketball growing up, and still do. I practiced basketball a lot, more than soccer when I was younger. After school, my brothers and I would be in our driveway until dinnertime when my mom would open the back door and yell at us to come inside. "OK, Mom, be right in!" Five minutes later she would yell again, this time with a lot more emphasis. "OK, Mom, on my way." Again, five minutes later she would yell last call. "OK, Mom, last

play. I swear." Another five minutes later, she would walk outside and threaten to give my dinner to the dog if I didn't come inside immediately because the food was getting cold. I wouldn't mess around this time. "Sorry, Mom, the game went to overtime so I had to finish it." I think over the years my mom learned to start calling my brothers and me fifteen minutes before the food was actually ready because she figured out that's how long it actually took for us to finally make it inside. (Thanks for the patience, Mom.)

Things got more serious when my dad "invested" in a Sport Court basketball hoop for the driveway. This thing was legit. Glass backboard with a handle in the back for raising and lowering—in other words, a nine-foot dunk setting. Dad even painted a three-point arc, free throw line, and key on the driveway. Even more amazing, he added two spotlights above the garage so we could play after dinner, too! Under the lights at night it was easy to pretend we were playing in an arena filled with thousands of people. I was in heaven.

So, at least during this stage of my childhood, I dreamed of getting a college scholarship to play basketball. Because both my parents went to Kansas State, we weren't the biggest Kansas Jayhawk fans at the time, so I imagined myself as Ed Cota, point guard for North Carolina, when I was on offense. When I played defense, I was Steve Wojciechowski, point guard for Duke. You might remember him for his hustle and how he used to get down and slap the floor.

I also dreamed about playing high school basketball. My dad would take me to big games around the city so I could watch and study some of the area's best players. I remember following Pembroke Hill with JaRon and Kareem Rush. There was also a big tournament I looked forward to every year at St. Thomas Aquinas with teams from around the Midwest. This is where I got to see David Lee from Chaminade out

of St. Louis. I've still never seen, in person, a high school player dunk like David Lee. I actually met him a few years ago in New York, and I told him about that tournament! He said he remembers it (he thinks).

Anyway, fast-forward to sophomore year of high school basketball tryouts. I was really excited for the upcoming season. We had a chance to be good, and I had a decent chance to get some minutes for the varsity, a dream of mine as a kid.

Unfortunately, I had one major issue: our head coach. He was an old-school Bob Knight kind of guy who never thought anyone was tough enough. He had lots of rules, and it was his way or the highway. One rule was if you missed a practice, you missed a game. If you missed two practices, you missed two games, and so on. Didn't matter what the reason or excuse was—even if you were sick.

I had previously run up against this rule during my freshman season. I had a big soccer tournament over Thanksgiving and missed five practices in a row. So that meant I had to sit out five games in a row when I got back. It seemed a little harsh to me, but I sucked it up and got through it because I really wanted to be a part of the program.

Before my sophmore season I knew I had a much larger conflict coming up. I had been invited to a major youth soccer tournament in Italy scheduled right in the middle of basketball season, and this time it was for twelve days. That meant if our coach held true to his rule, I would miss twelve games. That was half the season!

My parents prepared me to go into the head coach's office and break the news to him before tryouts started. We felt this was the responsible thing to do, and by giving him the dates beforehand we hoped he might bend his rule for my "special" case. I was so nervous to walk in and tell him. I agonized over it all day at school. Finally, I worked up the courage and presented my case with as much conviction as an intimidated high school sophomore can.

"This is a really big tournament and an unbelievable opportunity. Not many high schoolers get to experience this. I would love to play soccer in college, and this tournament gives me a huge chance to be seen by coaches and scouts." I even had an official letter with a fancy seal from U.S. Soccer explaining how special this situation was. I ended my speech with something like, "Soccer is really important to me, but so is basketball. I would appreciate if you considered allowing me to go to this tournament without missing any games. I promise I will work extra hard to make up for the time I miss."

It didn't work. He didn't bend. He told me he wouldn't make exceptions for anyone. It also didn't help that he wasn't a very big fan of soccer. I was devastated. My parents actually met with him the next day to make their own appeal, but still our coach wasn't budging. So my parents and I had a decision to make. Should I continue playing or not? Together, we tried to weigh both sides. On one side, was it worth it to go through all those practices and put in so much time and effort without being able to play for half the season? On the other side, would I regret not playing?

After a lot of stressful discussions, I made my decision that it wasn't worth it. A major factor that influenced my decision was that, more than likely, I would be facing similar soccer commitments my junior and senior years, and I didn't want to keep getting penalized and going through the same stress each season.

So just like that, my basketball career was over. I went into my coach's office with my parents for the last time to inform him of my decision. It was, in a word, terrible. I've never cried harder in my life, and by the time the brief meeting was over, my parents were in tears, too. (No doubt because of seeing the pain I was in.)

That was one of the most stressful and disheartening experiences I had ever been through. But life went on, as it always does. I ended up going on the soccer trip to Italy and had an unforgettable experience. Our team, which represented U.S. Region II ODP, was extremely talented and ended up winning the tournament. Every member from that team ended up playing Division I soccer and a handful (Tim Ward, Brad Ring, and Will Johnson) went on to have professional careers. Another teammate, Michael Bradley, became the captain of the U.S. Men's National Team.

It's easy to say now that things worked out, but at the time I was hurting. I felt like basketball was unfairly taken away from me, even though I was the one deciding to quit. I felt like I got cheated out of playing, all because I had interest in another sport. Our coach basically made me choose between soccer and basketball. Why couldn't I have played both? I practiced and prepared for basketball just as much as soccer. I had dreams in basketball just like in soccer, and they were gone in an instant with one decision. That's what hurts the most. I know that ultimately I made my own decision, but I honestly feel like I had no choice.

For the rest of high school, I tried to act like not playing didn't bother me, but it did. It was extremely hard to watch my old teammates get to play in front of all our classmates each Friday night during the winter. I was up in the stands cheering hard, but what I wanted most was to be out on the floor competing alongside them. It was especially tough my senior year when I had to watch our group of five seniors play together for one final season and not be a part of it.

With the passing of time, you gain perspective. To be fair, our basketball coach was an excellent coach and a very respected teacher of the game. He got the best out of his players and instilled a lot of good values. But I still haven't forgiven him for not changing his rule. Each time I run into him, I remind him how he forced me to choose between basketball and soccer. His response: "Well, if I would have known you would become a professional soccer player . . ." Yeah, yeah, yeah . . . I guess hindsight is always 20/20.

So this message is for kids: If you haven't already gone through something like this, you will. In today's sports landscape, there's a crazy amount of pressure being put on you to specialize in one sport. I don't know when exactly it will come, but at some point, you will be faced with a similar decision. You will feel pressure from other people. Each situation is different, but prepare yourself now to face it. In the moment, you might feel trapped, like there's no good way out. But as long as you are honest with yourself and make the decisions *you* want, things will work out.

It's OK to stand firm to a coach and respectfully say you want to play multiple sports. It's also OK if you decide to specialize and give something up. I'm just trying to help you understand that you don't have to give up something if you don't want to. And seriously, if your coach is giving you a hard time, you have my permission to tell my story. I've made it to a very high level in soccer, but I still regret giving up basketball when I did, and I don't want you to regret giving up an activity you love because someone pressures you to do so. You only have a small window to play sports in your life. Don't let anyone else slam it shut!

AUTHOR'S NOTE: *Both of my younger brothers played under the same coach. A couple years after I stopped playing basketball, my younger brother Mike helped lead his team to its first and only basketball state championship. Fortunately for Mike, he also excelled in football, which didn't have the seasonal conflicts that soccer does. However, a few years behind Mike, my youngest brother, Nick, went though the same exact situation I did. The outcome? Coach made an exception to his rule and allowed my brother to only miss two games. Therefore, he got to play his senior year. I'm so happy they both got to have those experiences.*

FREQUENTLY ASKED . . .

The question I get asked most from parents is, "What's one piece of advice you would give to a young player?"

The answer isn't simple. It depends on many different factors: age, goals, ability, resources, and others. So, let's consider age, and break that down into three categories. And keep in mind, there's a ton of advice I would give to young players, but since the question is "one piece of advice," I'll get right to what I believe is most important and relevant. Also remember that even though my experience is in soccer, a lot of what I'm talking about relates to other sports, too.

ELEMENTARY SCHOOL PLAYERS
Work on technique. For soccer players, this means dribble, pass, shoot. Learn how to juggle.

IN ELEMENTARY SCHOOL . . .
Spend time with the ball. Learn what you're good at. Go to YouTube and watch highlights and great moves, and then go out in the backyard and try to pull them off. This is the time to have fun . . . and to practice with your weak foot!

Practice volleying. Build a base foundation for years to come. If you can get your technique down at this age, you'll have a head start in everything else the game requires.

Specifically, practice everything with both sides of your body. I can't tell you how important this is. Most kids only practice with their strong foot. I get it. It's more fun to play with your strong foot because you're better with it. Why would you want to go out in the backyard and shoot with your weak foot and maybe score one out of five when you can shoot with your strong foot and score four out of five? But don't neglect your weaker side. This is the biggest mistake that young players make.

Learning to use the weak foot is like learning a new language. It's so much more difficult going back to learn when you're older. Believe me, I learned this the hard way. I always heavily favored my left foot growing up. Coaches and teammates used to joke that I only used my right foot to stand—that I had a peg leg. At those lower levels, I could get away with it, but that all changed in college. It became glaringly obvious that if I wanted to progress like I hoped, I needed to play with both feet. So after my freshman year at Notre Dame, I dedicated an entire summer to it. I played only with my weaker foot. Rep after rep, always with my right, never with my left. It's gotten a lot better, but it's still something I continue to work on to this day. And I sure wish I had learned at an earlier age how important it was to have equal strength and skill with both feet.

MIDDLE SCHOOL PLAYERS

Coordination, speed, agility, fitness, flexibility. . . . Around this time, your body is going to be changing. You're probably going to start growing, maybe fast. This is when

IN MIDDLE SCHOOL . . .
Diversify your activities. Ask your parents if you can try another sport or activity. Sign up for a fitness boot camp or speed and agility camp. This is a great time to develop athleticism and figure out your body's strengths and weaknesses. Remember the more well rounded you are, the better off you'll be.

"I FIGURE PRACTICE PUTS YOUR BRAINS IN YOUR MUSCLES."

—Sam Snead, golfing legend

it starts getting important to teach your body how to be strong, fast, and coordinated. Start adding some physical agility and fitness drills into your weekly routine.

I'm not saying you need to be in the weight room all the time—or even at all. There's so much you can do without weights that will help you develop strength and coordination. Balance drills are great. You should be stretching every single day. That's another mistake I made. I wish I had started stretching at a younger age and so does my body! Middle school's the time to develop a habit of stretching that will stay with you forever.

It's true that some kids are naturally more coordinated and maybe even more talented than others, but fitness is something you have full control over. That's why it's so important to start putting time and effort into your fitness at this age. There's nothing holding you back from getting fit. All you have to do is work at it. If you do, you're going to set yourself up for success by giving yourself another advantage over someone else. Don't underestimate the value of being fit. It's something a coach immediately notices about a player. Sometimes the first impression is the only one you get to make. Don't blow it because you didn't put in the work.

HIGH SCHOOL PLAYERS

This one I can answer in one word: **GRADES**. (Parents, you're welcome.)

You may be surprised that I didn't say something related to soccer. But in high school, the most important aspect of going on to play college soccer—or any sport—is grades. Again, I didn't realize this until my junior year when I went through the recruiting process myself. Fortunately, I had taken academics seriously my freshman and sophomore year, so I didn't have to worry. However, I had lots of friends and teammates who messed around their first two years of high school and didn't get good grades. Then when the time came to start getting recruited to play college soccer, it was too late. You can't go back and change your grades.

Don't make the mistake of thinking you'll be able to catch up. Start right away. Again, this is something you can control. Sure, you might not be able to get straight As. But I'm telling you, if you put in a decent amount of effort on class work, you will not have to worry about getting a chance to play in college. It's really unfortunate to see someone who has enough talent to play a sport at the next level, but not get that chance because of poor grades.

When I started getting recruited, the first question college coaches asked me was, "How are your grades?" The second question they asked me was, "How are your test scores?" Seriously. They didn't even ask me about soccer. Not until after I had told them my grades and test scores did we start talking about soccer. Once I told them I had good grades and I

IN HIGH SCHOOL . . .
Actively pursue your future. E-mail coaches of colleges and universities you're interested in and introduce yourself. Tell your high school teachers your plans and goals of participating in collegiate athletics. They might help you out and make sure you stay on track academically.

had taken the ACT and SAT, they would say, "Great! Now we can talk about soccer." This is how 75 percent of my conversations with coaches went. I couldn't believe it. I wish I would have known. But now I'm telling you, that's how it is. It's another aspect that you can control that will help give you an advantage over your competition.

BEING SMART WITH SOCIAL MEDIA

Social media is a part of most people's everyday life. For athletes, social media has really come into the spotlight the last few years. In my opinion, social media can be an enjoyable experience when used positively. However, be extremely careful if you decide to use it because it can also be very negative.

Before I get into any specifics, it's important to understand that social media is a choice. Even though social media has become the norm, don't feel pressured to make an account if you don't feel comfortable doing so. "Because everyone else does" should never be the sole reason for doing something.

It's also important to fully understand what you're doing. Make sure you know how Twitter, Facebook, Snapchat, and Instagram work before you start posting. Make sure you realize the dangers that go along with each platform.

Something I heard during a social media seminar for athletes has always stuck with me: "Social media is like a gun. Smart people will use it as a useful tool. Not so smart people will shoot themselves in the foot with it."

When I first started using social media earlier in my career, I thought it was a fun way to share my opinions and thoughts. I also liked the opportunity to engage with fans, to connect with them, and to hear their stories as well. Most of my experiences were positive, and I truly enjoyed using it.

Through social media, I've connected with people in ways that wouldn't be possible otherwise. I've met fans of all ages from all over the world, been inspired by their stories, been invited to season ticket holders' weddings and graduation parties, and wished A LOT of people happy birthday! I hosted a week-long scavenger hunt through Kansas City with prizes at each stop. We've also raised money for a lot of great causes from online auctions. I could go on and on.

Considering all these positives, it's easy to see why social media has become such a ubiquitous part of our lives. However, it's important to understand that social media also has another side—a much tougher, darker side.

In the last few years, it seems that social media has become a much more negative place. Sure, social media platforms are still a place to connect, to share, and to laugh, but more frequently, they have become a place to criticize and to attack. And even though I see far more positive comments in my own feeds than negatives—I'd say 80 percent positive to 20 percent negative—the positives can still get drowned out by the ugly nature of some negatives. They're the ones that stand out and the ones that

stay with you. And if someone says they don't mind reading nasty things about themselves, they're lying. We are all human, and no one enjoys being disrespected.

My intention isn't to scare you off from using social media, but to help you realize the challenges and dangers that come along with using it. I want you to understand that because it's the Internet, anonymous people are going to say things to you and about you that they would never say to your face. The negative comments are something you'll inevitably encounter and you'll have to figure out the best way to respond, which might simply mean not responding at all. A key skill for today's athlete is the ability to ignore and tune out the social media trolls. If you can, you'll be fine. If you can't, it might end up affecting your performance, your job, and your life.

At the end of the day, if you take one thing away from this section, make it this: Don't let social media become too much of a part of your life. Remember, it's just an app on your cell phone! It was invented for you to enjoy.

DOS AND DON'TS OF SOCIAL MEDIA

DO:

SUPPORT OTHERS

GIVE THANKS TO PEOPLE WHO SUPPORT YOU

SHARE NEWS

BE POSITIVE

BE LIGHTHEARTED

DOUBLE-CHECK YOUR SPELLING AND GRAMMAR

DON'T: BE NEGATIVE

BE DISRESPECTFUL

POST INAPPROPRIATE MATERIAL

SPREAD RUMORS

USE PROFANITY

POST AFTER MIDNIGHT

Remember to think before you post. The comments or photos you share online will live there a long time for prospective coaches, teammates, college recruiters, professional soccer clubs, or employers to see. Freedom of speech does not mean freedom from consequences!

BECAUSE I JUST DO (WHY I MAKE THE BED EVERY MORNING)

For most of my kid life, I asked questions (i.e., complained) about why I had to do certain chores. I had a tough time understanding the idea of them. Every time I was given a job around the house, I asked, "Why do I have to do this?" My parents always responded with, "Because you just do." Simple as that.

"Why do I have to mow the lawn if the grass is just going to grow again?"

"Because you just do."

"Why do I have to pick up my shoes if I'm just going to wear them again?"

"Because you just do."

"Why do I have to wash the dishes if we're just going to use them again?"

"Because you just do."

I must have heard this a thousand times. Until one day, when my mom gave me a response I will never forget. Actually, it was life changing. . . .

Most kids reach a point in life when they get tired of making their beds. My breaking point came when I was ten years old. One day, I just decided that the whole concept didn't make sense.

"Why do I have to make my bed if I'm just going to sleep in it again?"

I thought this was a valid point. My parents' reasoning—"Because you just do"—was no longer good enough for me. From then on, I was never going to make my bed again. I was free! So I stopped making my bed for a few weeks.

Until one day, my mom finally had enough. She came up to my room and firmly told me, "From now on, you will make your bed every morning. No questions asked."

I immediately responded, "Mom, why do I have to make my bed if I'm just going to sleep in it again?" I expected the typical response, "Because you just do."

Instead, my mom said, "Why do you wipe yourself if you're just gonna poop again?!"

Wow! I was totally caught off guard by that one. I quickly tried to come up with a clever answer, but all that slipped out was, "Because you just do."

My mom smirked at me, turned around, and walked out of my room. I couldn't believe it! Without even trying to, I proved her point—there are some things that just need to get done. They don't need a reason.

That's exactly what I learned that day. Don't try to rationalize everything you have to do. Just do it. Get it done.

As a side note, sometimes when I make my bed now, I think about . . . well, you know.

Thanks Mom.

"If it were up to me, I would make a living playing soccer forever. Unfortunately, the reality is my playing career is a short window in my life. Players must realize this, and be prepared for life after soccer."

Extra Time

FATHERHOOD, GIVING BACK, AND LIFE AFTER PRO SPORTS

"People always use that term 'game changer.' Having your first child... now THAT'S a game changer."

—MB 5

BELIEVING

I know religion can be a sensitive subject, but I appreciate the fact that different people hold different beliefs. I definitely will not tell you what I think is right, wrong, or true to me. However, religion plays a role in my own life, therefore I felt empowered to include this personal story.

isn't the case. Having a baby is truly a miracle. It's one of God's most impressive masterpieces.

Amanda and I tried to get pregnant for a couple months with no success. Despite this very humbling experience, we stayed positive and eventually received great news from the home

"Be thankful. Be appreciative. Someone else is praying for the things you take for granted."

—Anonymous

I believe in angels.

When my wife and I decided to start a family, we began the process like most young couples—extremely naively. I assumed you snapped your fingers, got pregnant, then waited nine quick months for the baby to arrive. I quickly learned this

pregnancy kit . . . positive! We were so excited. We both hopped on the phone right away and called our parents to tell them. I then made a call to our team doctor to share the news, and asked him what the next steps were. Remember, I had no clue what I was doing.

He congratulated us and set up an appointment at the doctor's office the following week.

Unfortunately, we never made that doctor's appointment. Just a few days later, we lost the baby. Even though it was at a very early stage, it was still devastating. I've never felt so disappointed before. In that moment, I had no idea what to do. I tried my best to console Amanda, but nothing I could say would make it better. We both felt lost and defeated.

During that time, we were also in the process of building a house. We knew we wanted to start a family, and our old house didn't have enough bedrooms for kids. Often, in the evenings, we would drive over to our new home's lot to see the construction progress. By that time, the construction of the house was also pretty much completed. The building crew had just cleaned up the lot and leveled it, leaving nothing in the yard except for dirt.

The day we lost our baby, I thought a trip over to our new house might help get our minds off everything. Plus, a crew had just put down sod, so I thought it might be fun to walk around the fresh new yard. As we pulled up, it started raining. Amanda decided to stay in the car, but I got out to walk through our new yard for the first time.

Just as I was about to head back to the car, something on the ground caught my eye. I reached down and picked up a small baby angel statue from the grass. At the time, I didn't think much of it, but I did think it was bizarre to find something like that in the middle of the yard, considering that the lot had just been cleaned up and sodded. How the heck did this tiny statue end up on top of the sod like that? There was nothing else in the yard. Anyway, I put the baby angel in my pocket and walked back to our car.

When I got back in the car, I showed Amanda what I had found. It hit both of us at the same time. *A baby angel statue?*

No way. On the same day we lost a baby due to a miscarriage? This must have been a sign from God. There's no other way to explain how something like that randomly appears in your brand-new yard.

It's hard to express how much that mysterious little statue helped us get through that difficult time. It opened our eyes to God and made us lean on Him for help. Once we found the baby angel, we prayed every single night for God to watch over us. After several weeks, Amanda had recovered enough that we could try to get pregnant again. The very next month, when Amanda took the home pregnancy test, it turned out positive.

This time, we made it to the doctor's appointment. And roughly nine months later, we welcomed our daughter Parker Rhea Besler into the world.

Finding that angel in our new yard left us with so many questions. How did it get there? What does it mean? Why did I find it that particular day? I expect those questions will never be answered. All I know is I truly believe God sent us an angel that day. It was in the form of a baby statue. I know this because I felt it. Amanda believes the baby we lost that day went up to heaven and came down into our yard to let us know he or she will be watching over us.

As I write this, our beautiful baby Parker is three months old. The baby angel statue stands on a shelf in her room, watching over her. It will be many years before Parker understands the significance of that little statue in her room, but someday she will. As for Amanda and me, we'll never look at that mysterious angel without thinking about the importance of faith and the power of God's love.

A CRAZY PERFECT
FORTY-EIGHT HOURS

When people say having their first child is the most amazing experience, they're right. Unfortunately, I wasn't able to be present for the event.

Let me explain. When I got called to the U.S. Men's National Team for our World Cup qualifiers at the beginning of September 2016, my wife Amanda was due with our first child two weeks later. However, considering these were two very important games, our country needed to win one of them to ensure our qualification into the next round (the Hex), and it was statistically unlikely our baby would come early, there was never a question of whether or not I should go.

Of course, there was always a chance our baby could arrive early and Amanda would go into labor while I was away. But it was just a chance. The greater chance was

I would play in both games, we would win them, then I could go home and our baby would arrive two weeks later, right on schedule.

We reasoned that on the *outside* chance Amanda's water broke while I was on the trip, I was only a phone call away. Our plan was to have our team's travel agent on standby so I could immediately book a flight home and make it back for the delivery. There's an old saying I've learned since then: "We plan. God laughs."

The first few days of camp were fairly uneventful. I would check in with Amanda in the morning, go to practice, check in again after lunch, and once more after dinner before she went to bed. We laugh about it now, but each time my phone rang and I saw it was from Amanda, my heart started racing and I answered the phone in a panic. I immediately thought she was calling me to say she was going into labor. To resolve this, she had to start each phone conversation with, "Hi, I'm not going into labor." Then I could relax, and say, "OK, good. So what's up?"

A few more days came and went like this, until our team traveled down to St. Vincent and the Grenadines (SVG), site of the first game. I had never been to SVG before, but we were informed this was a very small country. And the amenities we were used to such as Wi-Fi and cell phone service were going to be scarce. Also, access to this island was tough, so traveling in itself was a challenge. With all this in mind, our team decided to spend the least amount of time possible in SVG. Our plan was to fly in two days before the game, and leave immediately after.

When I boarded the final flight to SVG, it was the first time I became nervous about Amanda being pregnant. I made one last call to Amanda while my phone still worked and luckily she helped ease my apprehension. "I'll be fine. Don't worry about me. You'll only be down there for two-and-a-half

days. That's a small window."

Once we arrived at our hotel in SVG, I was able to keep my mind off everything back home by focusing on the game and trying to enjoy the experience of being in a country I'd never visited before. After a long day of travel, I fell asleep without any trouble.

The next day we had practice at **11:00 a.m.**

At **2:00 p.m.**, when I got back from practice, I saw I had a few missed calls from Amanda. Also, a text from her that said, "Call me ASAP." Oh boy, I thought. Surely this can't be happening right now. I called her back and the first thing she said to me was, "I think my water broke." I responded, "What do you mean you think your water broke? Are you sure?" She told me what happened and how she called the doctor right away to confirm. Sure enough, her water broke. Amanda was on her way to the hospital to get induced into labor.

In that moment, I was actually, surprisingly, calm. Because I wasn't there, I don't think I quite grasped what was going on. It all seemed a bit surreal to me. I remember sitting on my bed for a few minutes trying to process the information.

After a few seconds, I snapped out of it and realized I needed to get up and act. I needed to make it home! So I got up and ran over to our team administrator's office to tell him I needed a flight home. He said he would get to work right away and get back to me within the hour.

At **3:00 p.m.**, I went back to our administrator's office to check on the status of my flight. He told me it wasn't looking good. The fastest possible route would get me back to KC in thirty-three hours. Thirty-three hours? Are you kidding me? There had to be something else. We looked into everything—planes, boats, cars, you name it. One of my teammates even reached out to a private jet company via social media, explaining my situation to see if they might be able to help. (They never responded, but thanks for trying, Omar!) The problem was the island we were on was almost impossible to get to. The most popular way to get there was to take a four-hour boat ride from Barbados. Another way was to hop on a rinky-dink prop plane and fly over to Barbados, but there was only one flight each day and I had already missed it. Once I got to Barbados, my best option was flying direct to Miami, then to Atlanta, then home to Kansas City.

I called Amanda to fill her in on the situation. I told her the fastest possible way for me to get home would put me into KC in thirty-three hours (plus an hour drive to the hospital from the airport). When I told her this, I could sense the disappointment in her voice. In a time when she needed me by her side the most, I couldn't have been farther away. It felt like I was stuck on Mars and there was no way to get back home. It's hard to go back to this moment and think about how Amanda must have felt. I can't imagine how scary it must have been driving yourself to the hospital, having never given birth before, without your husband who was supposed to be there. On the phone, all I kept saying was how sorry I was that we were in this situation.

Basically, the two options I had were to leave as soon as possible and arrive home in thirty-three hours, or I could stay and play the game the following day, and leave on the team's charter flight the next morning, which would put me in KC about forty-five hours later. (The team's charter went from SVG to Barbados, then Barbados to Jacksonville. I would then break off from the team and fly on my own from Jacksonville to Ft. Lauderdale, then Ft. Lauderdale to KC.)

I spent about fifteen minutes on the phone discussing my options with Amanda. I kept telling her I was going to leave right away to come see her. She kept telling me to stay and play the game since I couldn't make it back for the actual birth. (I wouldn't make it in time for the birth because once her water broke, she needed to deliver within twenty-four hours.) Plus, she felt more comfortable with me staying with the team and traveling back on our charter flight rather than trying to travel all that way on my own.

Looking at it logically, I knew she was right. And she ultimately convinced me that the more responsible option was for me to play the game and fly back the next morning. I remember her saying, "If you can't make it back to help me through the birth, you should just stay. Once she's born, what's another twelve hours of waiting for you to meet her?" She also assured me that her mom would be right by her side the entire time.

Realization settled in. For what-

ever reason, I knew it wasn't part of God's plan. I was devastated. Amanda and I had waited almost ten months for this moment, and I was going to miss it. While Amanda was pregnant, I joked with her about not reading the baby books and skipping the birthing classes since I would likely miss the birth because I would be on the road for soccer. But I swear it was just a joke! There's no way I thought I would actually miss it. Karma sucks.

Our conversation left me a bit overwhelmed and discouraged. I wanted to pout. I wanted to scream. It didn't seem fair to me that I couldn't make it back. For a bit, I found myself complaining to Amanda, feeling sorry for myself, trying to get sympathy from her. Then I quickly realized I was being an idiot. What was I thinking? Why should Amanda be on the phone trying to comfort me for missing our child's birth? SHE needed comfort from ME. Not the other way around. She needed me to be strong for her. When I realized this, I decided to "man up." Instead of pouting and feeling bad for myself, I put all my focus on Amanda and our baby. Despite not being able to physically be there, I was going to do everything possible to help comfort Amanda. Together, we would find a way to get through the situation and make the best of it.

It was **4:00 p.m.** Our conversation had taken about an hour. When it was finally decided I would be staying, I walked out of my room and into my villa's common room where my roommates Graham Zusi and Omar Gonzalez were sitting. I said, "Well guys, sounds like I'm stuck here and going to miss the birth of my first child. I'm going to need your help to keep my mind off things and calm me down until she's born." Fortunately, they did exactly that. In a time when my anxiety and nerves were at an all-time high, they found a way to be there for me and help me get through a tough situation. I already knew it beforehand, but that day confirmed that they are truly great friends. We ended up playing cards, listening to music, and talking about anything and everything for the rest of the night. Omar in particular was a huge help. He has two daughters; as an experienced veteran, he was able to talk me through everything. I gave them updates each hour and asked what certain terms meant.

"She's dilated to a four now. What does that mean?!" Omar was always right there to answer.

The rest of the evening was a bit slow, if you can believe that. I checked in with Amanda each hour to get updates. Things were progressing on schedule and the doctors were just waiting for the right time for Amanda to start pushing.

By **11:00 p.m.**, I was surprisingly getting sleepy. I knew I needed to get at least a little bit of rest considering I was playing in a World Cup qualifying match the next day, a 1:00 p.m. kickoff. Amanda convinced me (again) that I should get some sleep. She told me it would be at least another few hours before anything happened, but as soon as something started she would call me to wake me up. I agreed, and somehow dozed off.

At **3:00 a.m.**, I woke up to my phone ringing. It was Amanda's mom. Amanda was dilated enough to start pushing soon. She handed the phone to Amanda, I told her good luck and how much I loved her, and Amanda's mom told me she would call back when everything started. When this happened, it was impossible to sleep. It was already hot and humid in my room, but I started sweating even more. I did everything possible to stay calm. I was in a room by myself, staring at the ceiling, taking deep breaths, and praying that everything would go smoothly.

Amanda's mom called at **4:00 a.m.** to tell me she officially started pushing. Our baby would be here soon! Now, I was out of bed, pacing back and forth. I remember looking out my window and noticing how bright the moon was. It made me feel really far away from Amanda. Every five minutes I would look down at my phone to see if I still had service, or if somehow I had missed a call. Time was going by so slowly. I couldn't handle the suspense. I called back to check, but there were no real updates. Amanda was still pushing.

Amanda was still pushing at **6:00 a.m.** And I was still pacing. I was trying to picture what was going on back at the hospital, but it was almost impossible. I started wondering how Amanda was doing and thinking about the different calming techniques I learned in birthing class that I was supposed to be using with her at that moment.

(They were meant for her, but I wondered if they'd work on me!)

At **7:00 a.m.**, I got a FaceTime call from Amanda. I was surprised because for most of the trip, I didn't have a strong enough Wi-Fi connection to access the Internet and FaceTime. I guess the Internet God was looking out for us. When I pressed accept, I immediately heard loud noises. Screaming, pushing, crying, talking, laughing, basically chaos. But what I saw was amazing. It was our baby girl being born. I watched our doctor deliver her and then place her into Amanda's arms. Amanda was crying with joy.

Parker Rhea Besler was born on September 2, 2016, at **7:06 a.m.** weighing seven pounds, four ounces, and measuring twenty and a half inches long.

I said "hi" to my baby for the first time and we talked (Amanda and I) for a few minutes before Parker went for infant tests. I told Amanda how proud I was of her and I loved her. What an amazing experience! I remember asking too many questions because I wanted to know everything. Amanda was exhausted and too tired to answer any of them. We both agreed to check in again in an hour.

By **8:30 a.m.**, the rest of my teammates were awake and we all had breakfast together. The news spread fast, and I was congratulated by each of my teammates at breakfast. I made sure to speak with our head coach, Jürgen Klinsmann, to assure him that I would be ready to play in our game a few hours later. I knew he trusted me, but I didn't want him worrying about my mental and physical state. It felt good speaking with him. I could sense his happiness for me in his reaction. He said, "Let's go out and handle business this afternoon in honor of your daughter. Then we'll get you home to meet her!"

On the drive to the stadium, I could sense it was going to be a special day. I kept looking out the window and couldn't stop smiling. My life became more complete earlier that morning. I felt like going to play a soccer game was so fun. Everything just felt right that day. It was tempting to be disappointed that I wasn't able to physically be back home with Amanda, but I took a different approach. I was on a mission to make the best out of this situation. It was already the best day of my life. Why not make

it even better? Plus, how many people get the opportunity to represent their country in a World Cup qualifier the same day they become a dad? Sure, it was unlucky I missed Parker's birth, but I was also lucky to have this opportunity. I was motivated to go out and play for Parker that day. I knew this day was going to be one I remembered for the rest of my life. My plan was to go out and play my tail off and score a goal for Parker. . . .

And that's what I did.

When I scored, I immediately thought of Parker. I couldn't believe it. Well, honestly, I could. Like I said, I had a feeling something special was going to happen in the game that day. Sure enough, I scored my first international goal for the United States. Right after the ball hit the back of the net, I turned around to see my teammates running over to celebrate with me. We all embraced and did a spontaneous "rock the baby" celebration to honor Parker. I could see how happy they were for me, and I'm so thankful they treated me the way they did. We actually never talked about doing the celebration; it just happened naturally. It's one of my favorite moments ever on a

soccer field. There's a picture that captured that celebration now hanging up on our wall at home.

The rest of the game, I was on a high from the goal and, even more, on a high from my daughter being born. Despite only getting a few hours of sleep, and probably being emotionally and mentally exhausted, I never got tired in the game. Adrenaline is such a powerful tool you can use. I definitely took advantage.

When I walked off the field that day, I knew I had just experienced something truly special. I knew I had missed the birth of my first child and I could never go back and change that. But I made the most of it, and I turned it into one

heck of a story. I can't wait until Parker is old enough to tell her the story about the day she was born. And if for some reason she doesn't believe her dad, I'll show her the article about it in the *New York Times*. Yep, that's right—Parker made the *New York Times* at one day old . . . She's famous!

After showering and getting changed, I stood in front of the media and did a live interview on camera that was being broadcast back in the United States. I had no idea if Amanda and Parker were watching (they were), but it didn't matter. During the interview, it didn't feel like I was talking to a reporter like it always does. It was more than that. It felt like I was speaking to my wife and newborn daughter back home. I looked into the camera and told them how excited I was to see them. I get chills thinking about how it felt when I looked into the lens and said, "I'll see you soon, Parker. I love you!"

At our team dinner back at the hotel, I was presented the game ball from our captain, Michael Bradley. I had everyone sign it, and I wrote Parker's name and birth information on it. I slept with the ball in my bed that night, and I was so excited to get back home to present it to her. I wasn't sure if I was going to be able to sleep that night because I was so anxious to get home, but I ended up sleeping like a baby (pun intended).

The trip home seemed to take forever. We left the hotel early in the morning with the team. After an hour-long bus ride and four separate flights, I finally landed in KC at **7:00 p.m.** I spent the entire day thinking about what it would be like to hold Parker for the first time. Also, I didn't let her game ball leave my grasp. My luggage didn't matter to me, only that

ball. I white-knuckled it the entire way. I kind of hoped I would end up sitting next to that person on the plane who talks the whole time and asks you your life story (never thought I would say that) just so I could brag and tell them about what just happened to me. But it wasn't meant to be, so I just slept.

After landing, I got into my car to drive to the hospital, and I suddenly became really nervous. I was trying to wrap my head around the fact that I was about to meet my baby. I had a knot in my stomach, like I was embarking

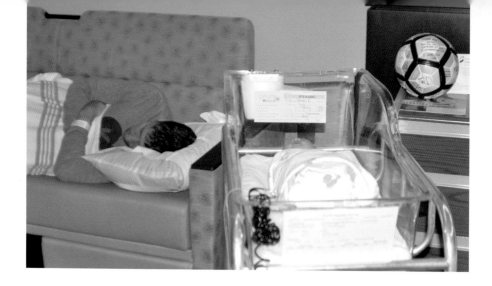

on an incredible journey and there was no turning back. As a defense mechanism, I usually combat nerves with humor. That's why I called Amanda and made the joke, "OK, I'm on my way to the hospital . . . this is my last chance to make a run for it. I might just take the wrong exit!" Obviously I was kidding, but it made us both laugh, which helped the drive go by a little quicker.

When I walked into the hospital room, I hugged Amanda and gave her a kiss, then she handed me Parker. I sat down on a chair and just stared at her. I was laughing and crying at the same time; I couldn't believe she was ours! She was amazing, so small and precious. I didn't move for thirty minutes, but finally put her down to sleep (because my arms got tired).

I sat down again, finally able to process everything that had happened in the past forty-eight hours. Once I made it back home and met Parker, it was all worth it. If I had to do it again, I wouldn't change a thing. Everything worked out exactly how it was supposed to, and I'm just thankful we were blessed with a beautiful, healthy baby. And if Parker ever tries to hold the fact that I wasn't there for her birth over my head, I'll just point out the game ball I earned for her that day. It's sitting in the corner of her room.

"Sometimes the littlest things take up the most room in your heart."
—Winnie-the-Pooh (A.A. Milne)

COMING
FULL CIRCLE

The feeling of becoming a dad is very hard to put into words. It's the proudest I've ever been. My cheeks hurt for a week after Parker was born because I couldn't stop smiling. The reality of it all definitely took a few days to sink in, but once it did, I felt more than just excitement and pride—I felt a little overwhelmed, and even humbled. For the first time in my life, I feel an enormous amount of responsibility for another human being. I know there are going to be challenges along the way, but I don't view them that way. I view them as privileges. It's a privilege to be her dad and I'm so grateful I get that opportunity.

One of the most rewarding experiences of becoming a dad was getting to see my parents' faces when they first held their granddaughter. When you're sitting together with three generations of family in a small hospital room, life really comes full circle. Our family instantly became closer. In this moment, I realized how lucky I was to have my mom and dad as my parents. They did such an amazing job, and I hope I can be just like them.

I've only been a parent for four months, but one thing I've already noticed is how much more I appreciate time. Before Parker was born, an hour to me was a long time. I could lie around and waste an hour with no problem. Now, an hour flies by. I seriously don't know where the time goes throughout the day. When I'm holding or playing with Parker, thirty minutes feels like three. I think I've learned to appreciate how precious time is and to never take for granted moments with your kid, because you'll never get them back.

"ANYONE WHO TELLS YOU FATHERHOOD IS THE GREATEST THING THAT CAN HAPPEN TO YOU, THEY ARE UNDERSTATING IT."

—Mike Myers

Bottom line, I'm really looking forward to the years ahead. Being a dad and raising a family is something I've always known I wanted to experience. I know there will be difficult moments, and I know I'm not going to get everything right the first time (or second, or maybe third). But I'm truly looking forward to it. I feel like I have deeper meaning in my life now, like being a dad is something I'm supposed to do.

ANOTHER KIND
OF ANGEL

Being involved in my community has always been a part of my life. I started when I was younger because my parents made it a priority, and it's carried over into my adult life. Back then, I didn't think much about what giving back meant, it was just something I did. And to be honest, a lot of times I did it because I had to. I had to volunteer at the soup kitchen because that's what my church did. I had to collect cans for Harvesters, a Kansas City food bank, because that's what my neighborhood did. I had to get a certain amount of service hours so I could get into my high school's National Honor Society.

Now that I'm older, I don't HAVE to do any of that . . . I WANT to. I want to give back. I want to get involved in the community. It's still a priority in my life. Here's a story from my rookie season in Kansas City that inspired me to make that choice.

I received an e-mail from Rob Thomson, vice president of communications at Sporting KC (then the Kansas City Wizards), asking if I had time to attend a girl's high school soccer game. The backstory was a sixteen-year-old girl playing for one of the teams had just come back from battling cancer and she was a huge soccer fan. Her name was Kori Quinn. Rob thought it would be a nice gesture if I attended her game and met her afterward to sign some autographs and take a few pictures.

I agreed with Rob and decided to attend. I drove out to Blue Springs High School, site of Kori's game, with Graham Zusi. We wore our Wizards gear and sat in the metal bleachers with all the parents. We watched Kori play and

"YOU CAN'T ALWAYS CHOOSE WHAT HAPPENS TO YOU IN LIFE, BUT YOU CAN ALWAYS CHOOSE YOUR ATTITUDE."

waited to meet her after the game. I was surprised at how talented a player Kori was. The way she was running around the field made it hard to believe she had just recovered from chemotherapy. When the game ended, Graham and I went down on the field to meet Kori and her teammates, and talked with them for a short while. I could tell they were all really nervous to be talking to two "professional soccer players."

I enjoyed getting to meet Kori. I remember driving home that night feeling good about volunteering our time to watch her game. I was definitely glad we went. But otherwise, I didn't think much more about it.

A few months later, I met Kori again. This time it was at a Sporting KC calendar shoot for Braden's Hope, a nonprofit foundation that raises awareness and research funding for childhood cancer. Kori was one of the cancer survivors chosen to participate in the calendar. Because I'd previously met Kori, I asked if I could team up with her for the photo shoot. We spent a few hours together taking pictures (with puppies!) and getting to know each other better. I was inspired and moved as Kori told me her story about battling Ewing's Sarcoma. I was astonished at how calm she was while talking about such a difficult subject. She knew her soccer, too! When I drove home from the calendar shoot that day, I again felt good about the time I'd spent with Kori. I decided I wanted to keep in touch with Kori and help her in any way possible.

Over the course of the next few years, I spent time with Kori at a number of different appearances

which meant continued hospital stays and rounds of chemotherapy. But each time, she battled and beat it. Somehow, she still managed to graduate high school on time. Seeing Kori at her graduation party was amazing. Hearing her tell me, "I'm looking forward to going to college just like a regular kid" made me so happy and proud of her.

All these interactions with Kori inspired me, but one day in particular pushed it over the top. Kori was back in Children's Mercy Hospital undergoing treatment, and I went to visit her. When I walked in, I thought I was going to cheer her up and possibly provide her with a little boost. So I thought. I was completely caught off guard when Kori greeted me at the door. Typically, we sat and visited in her room, but this time would be different. She said, "I think we could make more of a difference today if we visited other kids. They might need a pick-me-up more than I do." I couldn't believe what I'd heard, but I wasn't going to question what Kori wanted, so off we went on a tour of the hospital.

Walking around the hospital with Kori that day was incredible. Whichever room we walked into,

and charity events. Each time, we learned a little bit more about each other. And each time, I walked away more impressed and inspired by her. I even got asked to be Kori's "date" for Prom. It was an honor to spend time with her and her group of friends—and also a lot of fun.

Throughout these years, her cancer came back multiple times,

Kori knew each kid by name. She put a smile on each kid's face the moment she showed up. To be honest, the kids didn't really care about me—they were happier to see Kori. She was a rock star! Halfway through the day, I asked Kori how she got the idea to do this. She said, "Well, I've been through this before, so I know what it's like. I just feel the obligation to help these kids who are going through the same thing I did. I know it's scary, but I want them to know they can beat it." Wow. I had to turn my head away when she told me this so she wouldn't see me tearing up.

There Kori was, a cancer patient herself, taking time out of her day to help brighten the lives of the other children in the hospital. She would have done anything to help the kids feel more comfortable. I doubt Kori realized it (I don't even think I did that day), but she was making more of an impact on me than I was on her. I was supposed to be the "famous soccer player" showing up and signing autographs, but she was the one making the real difference.

From that day on, I knew I wanted to be like Kori. I felt an obligation to make a difference.

If Kori could find the time and strength to do it, there's no reason I couldn't. That day, I realized I needed to be more than just a soccer player. I had a platform to help people, especially kids, and I was determined to use it.

A few months after her high school graduation, Kori's cancer returned. This time it was stronger than before. I know Kori fought like hell, but tragically the cancer won. When I heard the news, my heart sank. I was speechless. It wasn't fair. I was mad at myself because I never got to tell her how inspired I was by her and how much she meant to me. I wanted one more moment with her to thank her for everything she had done for me. Heaven gained an angel on February 11, 2014 . . . which is coincidentally my birthday.

Three years later, I still find myself thinking about Kori all the time. At certain times when life doesn't seem fair, and I want to complain, I stop and think about how Kori would respond. No matter what, she always had a positive attitude. She always found a way to make a difference in other people's lives. Thank you, Kori. I know you're still watching out for us all.

LOOKING DOWNFIELD: LIFE AFTER SOCCER

A lot of people ask me about my plans after soccer. I never give them a definitive answer—not because I've never thought about it, but because it's impossible to predict the future. I have no idea where I will be or what I will be doing in five, ten, or twenty years from now. No one does. We may have ideas and plans for what we would like to be doing, but there's never a sure thing.

The only thing I know for certain is that my playing career will come to an end. No one plays forever. Of course, I'm going to do everything possible to play for as long as I can, but eventually I will have to stop. And when I do, I will have to do something else with my life. The good thing is I've always known that I will have to be more than just a professional soccer player. My playing career will be a chapter of my life, not my entire life.

Throughout my career, I've gone back and forth on scenarios that interest me after playing. Right after college, I thought it would make sense to use my premed degree and get involved in sports medicine, possibly even go to medical school. There have also been times where I can see myself as a coach, so I can stay involved in the game and make an impact on other players. Most recently, I've found interest in the business world through outlets such as real estate and investing. So when I say I'm not exactly sure what I'd like to be doing when I'm done playing, I truly mean it.

HOW WILL I REPLACE THE COMPETITIVE EDGE?

One thing a lot of former players, in any sport, struggle with is filling the competitive void left by retiring.

To be honest, this scares me. I know that I am an extremely competitive person, and I'm currently able to fulfill that need through playing soccer. When that gets taken away from me, I am going to have to find ways to deal with it because nothing will ever compare to the competitive challenge of playing professionally.

I wish I had a better idea about how to approach this. I wish there was a guide for former professional athletes with suggestions and options on how to fill this competitive void, but as far as I know, there isn't. I do know that each player processes the reality of retirement in his or her own way, so each player must find solutions to this abrupt change of status.

Maybe I can play more golf! I know that's a popular activity for former professional athletes because it provides competitive situations. Although I'm not sure how my wife, Amanda, feels about this idea. I joke, but I seriously would like to play more golf when I'm done playing soccer. I've always enjoyed the peacefulness of being outside on a course and the skill and discipline it takes to be good. Sadly, with my demanding schedule,

I only get to play a few times a year. I would love to spend more time playing and working on lowering my handicap. Plus, I've never gotten a hole in one, which has always been a bucket list item for me!

FAMILY MAN

One thing I know for certain, when I'm done playing I'm going to focus on my family even more than I already do. As I write this, I will be entering my ninth season as a professional, with who knows how many more seasons to come. That's a lot of years of sacrificing. That's a lot of years of being on the road, missing weddings, birthdays, holidays, and family dinners. I can't tell you how many times I've told Amanda, "I'm sorry for being gone so much. Remember this lifestyle is only temporary. I promise when I'm done playing I won't miss anything."

I love how Ray Lewis explained this situation in his autobiography, *I Feel Like Going On*:

> That's the thing people don't realize about this game—it takes the life out of you. I don't mean it saps your strength or beats you down, although it does that,

too. I mean it takes you away from the life you're meant to be living. That's the trade-off. All that time in the gym, all that time in practice, all that time on the road—it pulls you from the people you love. You trade the game for family time . . .

COMMUNITY: BESLER FAMILY FOUNDATION

After I am no longer playing professional soccer, I know I'd like to continue volunteering in the community. I have been blessed with so many opportunities by playing soccer that I feel I owe it to God to try and give back as much as I can. Plus, I truly enjoy getting involved in the community and trying to make a difference. I'm lucky that, as a professional athlete, I have a large platform right now, but I don't want to stop volunteering just because I stop playing.

As of today, the Besler Family Foundation isn't focused on one particular cause. I've been fortunate enough to work with numerous organizations such as the Victory Project, Children's Mercy Hospital, Child Protection Center, KC Pet Project, and the Leukemia and Lymphoma Society.

I envision my family's foundation only getting stronger when I'm done playing. I hope it can last for generations.

CLEAR EYES, FULL HEARTS

Although I don't know exactly what my life will be like after soccer, I hope I'll be able to find success and happiness. Whether it's in the business world, on the sidelines of a soccer field, or in some other professional field I haven't even considered yet, I am confident that I'll find my way. I'm confident because I know that whatever I do, I will always maintain clear eyes and a full heart. If I can do this, I'll be more than OK. And so will you.

Always remember . . .

Clear eyes, full hearts . . . CAN'T LOSE!

APPENDIX: MY SCHEDULE AND FAVORITE WORKOUTS

MY GAME DAY SCHEDULE (7:30 P.M. KICKOFF)

8:00 a.m. Wake up

8:15 a.m. Small breakfast: Greek yogurt and fruit

9:00 a.m. Go for a walk around the neighborhood

9:30 a.m. Stretching routine

10:30 a.m. Breakfast: scrambled eggs, bacon, toast, smoothie, chocolate milk

11:00 a.m.–3:30 p.m. Relax with my feet up; go to a movie, watch sports, read a book

3:30 p.m. Pregame meal: salmon, broccoli, mashed potatoes, pasta

4:00–5:00 p.m. Pregame nap

5:15 p.m. Shower and dress

5:30 p.m. Leave for stadium

5:55 p.m. Arrive at stadium

6:15 p.m. Stretching routine in locker room

6:45 p.m. On field warm ups

7:30 p.m. Kickoff

9:30 p.m. End of game

9:45 p.m. Media availability

10:00 p.m. Shower

10:15 p.m. Postgame treatments and contrast ICE and HOT bath for twenty minutes

11:00 p.m. Shield club to meet with family, friends, and fans

11:30 p.m. Leave stadium

12:00 a.m. Get dinner (at wherever's open!)

12:45 a.m. Back home

1:00 a.m. Watch replay of game

3:00 a.m. Go to bed

MY DAILY SCHEDULE (NONGAME DAY)

7:00 a.m. Wake up

7:30 a.m. Breakfast at home: two hard-boiled eggs, Greek yogurt, clementine, water

8:00 a.m. Leave for training facility

8:20 a.m. Arrive at training facility

8:30 a.m. Second small breakfast: smoothie, granola bar, water, vitamins, fish oils

8:45 a.m. Shower

9:00 a.m. Correctives in the gym (Each player has deficiencies in their body's movements. Correctives are exercises that work to "correct" those deficiencies. Mine focus on ankle and shoulder mobility.)

9:15 a.m. Stretching routine

9:30 a.m. Activation (This consists of activating my core and glute muscles, which helps prepare my body for the upcoming training session.)

9:45 a.m. Team meeting to go over objectives for the day

10:00 a.m. Training on field

11:30 a.m. Cool down and stretch on field

11:45 a.m. Media session (answer questions from reporters)

12:00 p.m. Weights session in the gym (I cycle through total body, upper body, and lower body lifts, depending on what day of the week it is.)

12:40 p.m. Drink post-training recovery shake

12:45 p.m. Post-training stretching and foam rolling

1:00 p.m. Shower

1:15 p.m. Post-training treatments and ICE bath for ten minutes

1:45 p.m. Eat lunch

2:00 p.m. Leave training facility

2:20–3:30 p.m. Back at home: relax and put my feet up

3:30–5:00 p.m. Run errands or attend a community appearance

5:45 p.m. Start preparing dinner

6:30 p.m. Eat dinner (and dessert, of course): salmon or chicken, green vegetable, and potatoes or rice

7:15–8:00 p.m. Family time

8:00 p.m. Put Parker down for bed

8:15–9:15 p.m. Watch TV, Netflix, hang out, read, catch up on e-mails

9:15 p.m. Get ready for bed

9:30 p.m. Sleep

MY FAVORITE WORKOUTS

PYRAMID TREADMILL RUN

SPEED — 10.0 MPH

INCLINE — 6.0 %

  :20 SEC ON / :20 SEC OFF

  :40 SEC ON / :40 SEC OFF

  1:00 MIN ON/OFF

  :40 SEC ON/OFF

  :20 SEC ON/OFF

} 5 SETS

REST 2-3 MIN BETWEEN SETS

THE ORIGINAL "300" WORKOUT

- MUST COMPLETE EACH EXERCISE COMPLETELY BEFORE MOVING TO NEXT EXERCISE
- COMPLETE WORKOUT IN LEAST AMOUNT OF TIME AS POSSIBLE

- PULL-UPS 25 REPS
- BARBELL DEADLIFT 135 LBS. 50 REPS
- PUSH-UPS 50 REPS
- 24 INCH BOX JUMPS 50 REPS
- FLOOR WIPERS 50 REPS
- SINGLE ARM CLEAN + PRESS
  W/ 35 LBS. KETTLE BELL 50 REPS
- PULL-UPS 25 REPS

Shuttle Run

300 Yard Shuttle

- 2 cones 50 yards apart
- Down and back 3 times
- < 60 seconds
- 4 total sets
- 1 minute rest in between sets

100 Yard Shuttle

- 2 cones 25 yards apart
- Down and back 2 times
- < 15 seconds
- 6 total sets
- 45 seconds in between sets

Navy Seal Workout

Pull-ups	1	2	3	4	5	6	7	8	9	10
Push-ups	2	4	6	8	10	12	14	16	18	20
Sit-ups	3	6	9	12	15	18	21	24	27	30

- Start w/ 1 pull-up, 2 push-ups, 3 sit-ups
- Then 2 pull-ups, 4 push-ups, 6 sit-ups
- Then 3 pull-ups, 6 push-ups, 9 sit-ups
- Continue pattern until 10, 20, 30

* For an extra challenge, try going back down to 1, 2, 3 once you finish!

ACKNOWLEDGMENTS

Thank you to everyone who helped me along this journey. I would never have thought I would write a book, but here I am! Without you all, this project would not have been possible.

To Amanda, thank you for being my rock. I can't wait to read this book to our kids one day.

To Mom and Dad, thanks for contributing and helping me remember certain events in my childhood. Mom, thanks for going through the scrapbooks and providing so many photos.

To Jean Lucas, my editor, thank you for keeping me on track throughout this process. We couldn't have done this without your leadership and direction.

To Rob Thomson, thank you for inspiring me to write this book.

To Patrick Regan, thank you for teaming up with me and helping me every step of the way. I've enjoyed getting to know you and your family throughout this process, and you'll forever be considered a friend.

To the designer, Diane Marsh, and all the photographers who graciously contributed their work to this book, Matt Cashore, Mike Gunnoe, Gary Rohman, Nick Smith, and Whitney Summers, you helped bring life to my stories.

Finally, to all my teammates, past and present. Without you guys, none of this is possible. You're the reason why I have memories and stories to tell. You're the reason I have lessons and advice to give.

—MB5

PHOTO CREDITS

All photos are reprinted with the permission of the photographers listed below. Every effort has been made to identify the correct photographer. If an error or omission has been made, Andrews McMeel Publishing will correct it in a reprint.

Diane Besler: pages 8, 13, 15, 16, 22, 25, 28, 29, 31, 36, 39, 51, 129, 152, 172, 175, 176 (top and bottom left)

Matt Besler: pages 41, 187, 197, 198, 199, 204, 206

BPI, ISI Photos: page 101

Matt Cashore/Notre Dame University: page 176 (middle right)

Robert Cianflone, Getty Images: pages 4-5

John Dorton, ISI Photos: page 196

Paulo Duarte, Associated Press Images: page 126

Mike Gunnoe: pages 9 (top), 33, 42, 46, 78, 86-87, 92, 97, 102, 146, 156, 176 (bottom right), 177, 216

Sharaya Mauck Photography: pages vii, 7 (top left)

Denny Medley, USA Today Sports: pages 34-35

Gary Rohman: pages ii, iv-v, 32, 58-9, 68, 70, 84, 85

Thomas B. Shea, ISI Photos: page 176 (top right)

Nick Smith: pages 9 (bottom), 63, 65

Sporting Kansas City: page vi

Whitney Summers, Maylyn Photography: page 7 (top and bottom right), 201

John Todd, ISI Photos: pages 118, 127, 128

U.S Soccer: page 11

Andrews McMeel Publishing
a division of Andrews McMeel Universal
1130 Walnut Street, Kansas City, Missouri 64106
www.andrewsmcmeel.com

17 18 19 20 21 SDB 10 9 8 7 6 5 4 3 2 1
ISBN: 978-1-4494-7977-0
Library of Congress Control Number:
2017939291

Editor: Jean Z. Lucas
Creative Director: Tim Lynch
Art Director: Diane Marsh
Production Manager: Carol Coe
Production Editor: Maureen Sullivan

ATTENTION: SCHOOLS AND BUSINESSES
Andrews McMeel books are available at
quantity discounts with bulk purchase for
educational, business, or sales promotional use.
For information, please e-mail the Andrews
McMeel Publishing Special Sales Department:
specialsales@amuniversal.com.